CYBERSECURITY DESIGN

2 BOOKS IN 1

BUILDING SECURE RESILIENT ARCHITECTURE

BOOK 1
NETWORK SECURITY FUNDAMENTALS
SECURITY ARCHITECTURE & DESIGN PRINCIPLES
BOOK 2
IMPLEMENTING CYBERSECURITY RESILIENCE
PHYSICAL SECURITY CONTROLS & CRYPTOGRAPHIC CONCEPTS

RICHIE MILLER

Disclaimer

Every effort was made to produce this book as truthful as possible, but no warranty is implied. The author shall have neither liability nor responsibility to any person or entity concerning any loss or damages ascending from the information contained in this book. The information in the following pages are broadly considered to be truthful and accurate of facts, and such any negligence, use or misuse of the information in question by the reader will render any resulting actions solely under their purview.

Table of Contents – Book 1

Table of Contents – Book 2

4

BOOK 1

NETWORK SECURITY
FUNDAMENTALS

SECURITY ARCHITECTURE & DESIGN PRINCIPLES

RICHIE MILLER

Introduction

IT Security jobs are on the rise! Small, medium or large size companies are always on the look out to get on board bright individuals to provide their services for Business as Usual (BAU) tasks or deploying new as well as on-going company projects. Most of these jobs requiring you to be on site but since 2020, companies are willing to negotiate with you if you want to work from home (WFH). Yet, to pass the Job interview, you must have experience. Still, if you think about it, all current IT security professionals at some point had no experience whatsoever. The question is; how did they get the job with no experience? Well, the answer is simpler then you think. All you have to do is convince the Hiring Manager that you are keen to learn and adopt new technologies and you have willingness to continuously research on the latest upcoming methods and techniques revolving around IT security. Here is where this book comes into the picture. Why? Well, if you want to become an IT Security professional, this book is for you! If you are studying for CompTIA Security+ or CISSP, this book will help you pass your exam. Passing security exams isn't easy. In fact, due to the raising security beaches around the World, both above mentioned exams are becoming more and more difficult to pass. Whether you want to become an Infrastructure Engineer, IT Security Analyst or any other Cybersecurity Professional, this book (as well as the other books in this series) will certainly help you get there! But, what knowledge are you going to gain from this book? Well, let me share with you briefly the agenda of this book, so you can decide if the following topics are interesting enough to invest your time in! First, you are going to discover what are the basic security concepts in an enterprise environment such as configuration management, data sovereignty, data protection, and why we should be protecting data in the first place. Next, you will learn about geographical considerations such as site resiliency; and then also something referred to as deception and disruption. After that, you will understand the basics of virtualization and cloud computing. We'll be also talking about cloud models, managed service providers, and the concept of fog and edge computing. Next, you will discover how to secure microservices and APIs or application programming interfaces. We'll also talk about SDN and SDV, or software-defined networking and software-defined visibility. After that, we'll talk about serverless architecture, and virtualization. Next, you will discover how to implement secure application development and automation in various types of environments. We'll also going to cover testing, staging, QA and production, provisioning and decommissioning resources. We'll also cover integrity measurement and what that means, secure coding techniques and careful considerations and planning when coding for security. Next, we will cover OWASP specifications or the Open Web Application Security Project, along with software diversity, automation and scripting. We'll also talk about elasticity, scalability, and version control in various environments that we can deploy into. After that, you will learn about authentication and authorization methods and the various technologies associated with those. We'll also talk about smartcard authentication, biometrics, multi-factor authentication, or MFA deployment, as well as authentication, authorization, and accounting, otherwise known as AAA, as well as cloud, versus on-premise requirements, as far as authorization and authentication is concerned. If you are ready to get on this journey, let's first cover what are baseline configurations!

Chapter 1 Baseline Configuration, Diagrams & IP Management

First we are going to cover security concepts in an enterprise environment. If we take a look at what we have at a high level, we have security concepts in an enterprise environment such as configuration management; we'll talk about data sovereignty, what that means and some gotchas there potentially; we'll talk about data protection, the various methods, and why we should be protecting that data; and then geographical considerations; site resiliency; and then also something referred to as deception and disruption. Every organization, enterprise, company, regardless of size, has a need to maintain standards in some type of configuration management. There's a number of reasons for this. Number one, we want to standardize the environment. The more standardized something is, the easier it is to maintain, the easier it is to find anomalies and to troubleshoot. By doing that, we can set baselines within our environment and then understand what is normal. Because once we understand what's normal, it's much easier to figure out what's not normal, what stands out, what are red flags, etc. Another side benefit is to identify conflicts and collisions. When we have configuration management at scale and we have a number of different people groups, all needing to make changes, all needing to adjust configurations, and if we have some type of collision calendar or a configuration management calendar, whether we call it a change board or a configuration management process, if we all have our processes documented, and then we review that whether it's weekly or monthly or whatever your change schedule is, we review that to make sure that some changes are not going to step on each other, cause conflicts in some form or fashion, and it just lends itself to having the organization run that much more smoothly. To put it into a definition, configuration management is the management and control of configurations. Configuration management is the management and control of configurations for an information system with the goal of enabling. And here's the takeaways: enabling security and managing risk, because that's really what we want to do. We want to enable security. We want to make sure our environment is as secure as possible. But we also want to manage risk. We don't want to unnecessarily introduce risk into the environment. Conversely, the risk that is there, we want to be aware of it and understand how to manage it. We can accept it, we can transfer it, we can pass it on. We can just say that we're willing to accept that part. It's going to cost too much to remediate, and we're just going to accept it. There's a lot of different ways to handle it, but configuration management allows us to have that line of sight and that overall big picture to understand when things change, and the more standardized that is, the easier it is to see. But just understand the basics of configuration management. The method of determining what's normal, why do we do that? Well, changes can quickly be identified then. If we have a big environment, don't think, necessarily, maybe you have a small environment with only a few computers or a few servers, maybe a few hosts, very easy to see things when they change. Once you start to get into bigger environments and you have hundreds or thousands of servers or tens of thousands of servers, it's very, very difficult to manage the snowflakes. By standardizing, we can identify changes very quickly and we can roll them back if necessary. Patches and updates can also be determined very quickly, were they successful or did they fail? We can quickly determine a success or failure and then roll back if necessary. Also, changes throughout an enterprise are documented, discussed, and then any potential collisions determined. By having that collision calendar, we make sure we're minimizing risk. We're not introducing unnecessary risk into the environment, and we're making sure that changes can be applied successfully. At the end of the day, it doesn't matter if we can roll the change back or not. It's still a pain; it still requires time and effort and resources validation teams. If we can avoid that whenever possible, it just makes for a much more smooth running operation. One of the things that we want to do when we're doing configuration management is to diagram, to understand how things work. Diagramming visualizes how things work, how they're connected, and how they interoperate. It's very timely, and it helps us to visualize and then troubleshoot, and we can understand all the dependencies and how things connect. Dependencies are identified and they're documented, inputs and outputs are understood, security risks can be discovered and then mitigated, and then applications, networking, compute, storage, all of those things, we have line of sight as to how they connect, what's dependent on each other, etc. It's a very lonely day when you have an outage, and all of a sudden you didn't realize that 15 other applications actually depended upon that application that just failed. And when your boss or your boss's boss starts asking, what about this, what about that, what about that application, what about that application? And you have no idea that even connected or talk to each other, it doesn't look good. So by having all these things diagrammed, documented, it allows us to derisk the environment. Making sure that things are stable as they can be, that we can quickly remediate when things do happen, and the more standardized, the better we're going to be. In addition to diagramming, we also have something referred to as a baseline configuration. In a baseline configuration, setting those baselines is critical to quickly identifying changes and configuration drift. When I say configuration drift, I mean over time, little things get tweaked and changed, and it gets to the point where you can't even tell where you're at anymore, what was normal, because so many things have changed. Well, if we have a baseline that we can roll back to, then we can even programmatically, every so often, reapply, whether it's group policy or some script or something to the environment that will roll those things back, so that if someone adds in an administrator where they shouldn't have been or they make a change to a policy or maybe even within the registry or in a conf file, it just depends upon the environment, what operating system. But if those changes get introduced and we don't really want them, some rogue administrator decides to do a one-off just because he thinks it may make his life easier, well, when it comes time to remediate, that person may have left that department or that role 6 months or a year prior but now we have an issue with something that they changed and only they know about, it becomes very difficult to find that needle in a haystack. So by having baseline configurations, we periodically just apply to the environment and we keep things standardized. Also when hackers or bad actors in a system or a network, what do they want to do? They want to change things. They're going to try to install backdoors, persistence or elevate privileges. Those changes can be quickly discovered, or more quickly because they're outside of that norm or that baseline. So having those things in place makes it much easier to identify. In case you actually haven't guessed it yet, the name of the game is standardization. The more standardized things are, the easier they are to maintain, to deploy, and also to troubleshoot. I really want that to be a takeaway for you. And if you don't have a standardization policy or working toward that in your environment, I highly recommend that you do so. It will make your life easier. It will reduce outages and also make troubleshooting when there is an outage that much easier. Let's change gears slightly and talk about IP address schema. And when I say schema, I mean, what is your IP address plan? Going back to what I said before about standardization, a schema allows us to have some type of standardization, some conformity around how we actually allocate IP addresses. Standardize. And then also maintain an IP address database. To an extent, we do that with the DHCP. It maintains a scope and a database of IP addresses for us. But in a large environment where we may have multiple DHCP scopes, we may have multiple DHCP agents or relay agents and servers that are acting in that capacity, it's possible to have things overlap. Or it's possible to have things that are allocated an IP address and we just don't know what that thing is, who's getting the IP address. So part of that database should be allocations and also reclamations. When we allocate an IP address, we should document who it's allocated to. Then also when we reclaim that IP address, it should also be brought back into the pool and back into our database that reflects that reclamation. A toolset or a suite of tools that can do that for us to an extent, is IP control or IP address management, IPAM. Different organizations will refer to it as something different. It may not be called the same thing in your organization if you even have it. But IP control is a way for you to simplify management, make troubleshooting easier, and then also increases security. Because we can understand at a glance what our IP addressing scheme is, and so we have, like, say, servers allocated a certain range, hosts perhaps allocated a certain range,. We may have things broken off into VLANs, or virtual local area networks, like for management IP addresses. For now, just suffice it to say that it's important for us to standardize and then also increase security. Troubleshooting also becomes easier because we have a database we can look up very quickly and say, this IP address was assigned to so and so. That assumes that we have good information in, the old saying garbage in, garbage out. We have to make sure that we have mechanisms in place to keep these things updated. But assuming all things are in play and all things are working properly, it increases security and makes troubleshooting and management much easier.

Chapter 2 Data Sovereignty & Data Loss Prevention

Next, let's talk about data sovereignty. Sovereignty, means who owns the data. When data is stored electronically, and this is something that you may or may not be aware of, it is actually subject to the laws of the country in which it's located. If you store data outside of your own country, it's possible that that data is subject to a different set of laws than what exists in your existing or your own country. Some other countries may have more stringent access rules, meaning they can access or mine that data, and you may not necessarily want that. It's important to understand these things before you start putting data in other locations. Who owns the data and who has access? Also, who can mine the data or pull things out of it. Depending upon the country around the world, law enforcement, government agencies, some countries are very stringent and they want access to all of it. Others are less restrictive and more geared toward the actual consumer or the individual person and their privacy. But those same sets of laws and policies don't exist globally, It's important understand where that data sits and what rules or regulations it falls under. Laws governing data use, access, storage, and also deletion, will vary from country to country. When you store information in the cloud, make sure you understand how that data is actually being stored, does it replicate to other data centers, are these data centers in a specific region, or are the outside of the country? Typically, you'll be made aware of those things, but just something to keep in mind. Next, let's talk about data loss prevention, or DLP. DLP detects potential breaches and also, and more importantly, the exfiltration of data. A few ways this can actually be instantiated, we have endpoint detection, that means data that's actually in use, we have network traffic detection, so data that's in transit, if it's going from one location to another, could be internal. But typically, we're doing DLP when we're having data leave our network. If it's crossing our boundary and going out to the internet, many companies will have DLP infrastructure in place that will stop that data from leaving, inspect it first, and then if it meets that criteria, we'll allow that data to go outside of the network. If for whatever reason it's determined that that data is not applicable or not permissible to leave, then it just shuts down that communication and does not let that email or that communication to be sent. Then we also have data storage, or data at rest. We can have devices that will scan in any one of these formats. It may just scan data at rest to make sure there's not PII, or PHI, health information, sitting inside file shares, network shares that are not necessarily secure. It can pull that data out, alert the user and say we found XYZ in a file store in your name or that you're showing as the owner of, it had personally identifiable information or HIPPA related or PCI data. We removed that file from your file share. It's in this quarantined location. Please double-check on it if it's valid, pull out the information you need, otherwise it will be deleted, things along those lines. There are automated methods to alleviate some of the pain associated with having to scan a very large network. Some additional methods of data loss prevention would be USB blocking. Don't allow people to insert USB devices, thumb drives into their machines, copy data, and then leave. Also, we have cloud-based and then email blocking. A lot of these things, again, are an automated process. They can scan, they can do SSL interception, even if that data is encrypted, depending upon the organization and the devices that they have in play, they can do what was traditionally called a man-in-the-middle attack. Now it's an on-path attack. But have a piece of infrastructure that sits in between the end user and who they're communicating to, and it will actually intercept that SSL traffic, unencrypt it, pull all the information out, see if there's anything that might be compromising, and then stop that communication from leaving the network. When we're talking about types of data to secure, three main ones that I want you to be aware of. We have data at rest, as you might guess, is data sitting on a hard drive or removable media. It's local to the computer, or it could be remotely on a storage area network or network attached storage, SAN or NAS, but it's data that is sitting somewhere. Next, we have data in transit, that's data that's being sent over a wired or a wireless network. A VPN connection will encrypt that data while it's in transit, again, wired or wireless. But once it actually sits on the disk, that VPN does not encrypt that data. That's where you would need data at rest. And then we have data in use, so data that's not at rest, and it's only on one particular node on a network. It's in memory on that server. Could be memory, it could be swap or temp space, but it's being used or accessed at that point in time. Even data that's at rest encrypted, once an application, once the server or an application accesses that data, it unencrypts it, brings it into memory. There are different ways to encrypt these pieces of data, depending upon how sensitive they are, and it will vary from application, it will vary from institution, perhaps regulatory compliance issues as well. But just understand the three different types and where it may fit into your environment.

Chapter 3 Data Masking, Tokenization & Digital Rights Management

With data masking, what we're doing is hiding or obfuscating some piece of data, whether it is in a database or an application, we're hiding that from someone who's not supposed to have access to that component of data. We're giving them access to some of it, but not necessarily all of it. When we're talking about data masking, there's a couple different types. So data masking can be done within applications, databases, at the individual record, row, or the entire table. We can make pieces of data available so someone can use that to test, to try communication, to see how things may work, maybe a query or setting up a development database, maybe iterating through, making changes to some databases, some tables or some applications. They need some data to test to make sure it works. But they shouldn't have access to sensitive data, so we're masking part of that out. In another area, you may hear the term IP address masking - just giving you a few different types of definitions so you're familiar with them. With IP address masking, another term for that might be network address translation or NAT. What that does is, it enables private IP addresses, the IP addresses that are not routable out on the internet, it allows us to use those internally, but then have an IP address that's public facing that masks all of the internal IP addresses. It allows internal hosts right inside of a network to communicate with the outside world without requiring them to have a public IP address or even giving away their internal IP addressing scheme. From the outside world, it all looks like it's coming through that public IP address or that range of public IP addresses. And then also understand that data masking can be static or dynamic, so data at rest or data in transit, and it could be done in a variety of methods, encryption, substitution, nulling, or just zeroing out the data, tokenization. And we'll talk about to organization a little more detail here shortly. But just understand that there are a number of ways that we can hide that data or obfuscate that data from unauthorized viewing. As an example, here we have a database, we have a few databases running, a database engine, and that contains the raw data. That has the data that's actually sensitive and non-sensitive. We have a combination of different things. We have some line-of-business applications that need access to that data, but not necessarily all of it. Some applications or some lines of business may need access to everything; some lines of business may not need access to everything. They may not be authorized to view some of that. What we do is, we put in a dynamic data masking engine. This is one method of doing; it's not the only way. But it's a method that can be use. A data masking engine can be put in line in between the database and line-of-business applications. We couple that with a firewall and, in this case, a firewall with an IDS, or an intrusion detection system. We can then consider that the masked data. Those lines of business applications, when they need to access that data, it will go through the firewall, access a load balancer, and then that goes through the data masking engine so requests are handled appropriately. The applications that may need full access have it; the ones that don't get a subset, and that can be done through encryption, tokenization or nulling. Different systems, different platforms have different methods for doing that, but the end result is the same. As an example, one of those lines of business might do a query, might query the database. The unmasked query result will return good old Alice and Bob, our two old friends, but it also shows their Social Security number. That's a no-no for most areas within the business. There's no need to know that. Even though we have the data there, we don't want to make that data visible, or viewable, to certain lines of business, to certain users or groups. We also don't want to have to maintain separate databases with raw data and then the masked data. If we have to maintain multiple databases, then it becomes problematic to have things kept in sync, what's the actual source of truth. So by masking, we can maintain one database but then just mask the results. In this case, the masked query result would give Alice and Bob, that would either be encrypted or it could be replaced with something else, could be tokenized, and we'll talk about some of these methods in more detail here shortly. But just understand that the result is then unreadable to the person on the other side who's making that query. If they don't have access to that data, they don't get it. When it comes to data masking and tokenization, what we're talking about is this. A tokenization process is replacing sensitive data with a non-sensitive equivalent. The token can be single use, it can be multiple use, it can be cryptographic or non-cryptographic, meaning it's some type of cipher, or can just be replaced with something, maybe a one-time replacement. It can be reversible or irreversible. There's a number of methods to implement tokenization. Then there's two different types. We have high-value tokens, or HVTs. That can be used to replace things like primary account numbers, like PANs, on credit card transactions, and it can be bound to specific devices, so like for instance, an iPhone. It can be bound to that phone That your fingerprint or your face ID, that would be used, that's a tokenization of a credit card, the credit card information. Then we have low-value tokens. LVTs can serve similar functions, but those things actually need the underlying tokenization system to match it back to the actual PAN - a tokenization example. Let's walk through this. The customer makes a purchase and the token goes to the merchant. The merchant passes that token along to the merchant acquirer, the merchant acquirer passes that token over the network, which is all connected through the financial network, and that data then resides inside of a secure bank vault, an electronic bank vault, in this case. The token vault is consulted to match the token with the customer. It goes back now and actually contact the bank matches things up, makes sure that that token matches with the customer to make sure it's verified. From there, the bank passes it back and says we're good to go. The network passes the token and the PAN, or the primary account number to the bank. The bank verifies funds, and authorizes this transaction. The information is passed back through the network acquirer and to the merchant to complete the transaction. It seems like a lot of things happening behind the scenes, and it is. But if you think about how quickly that actually happens in real life, you go to a point of sale terminal, you pull out your phone, whether it's Android or iOS, and you simply put it up to the card reader, it goes click and verified and the purchase is made that quickly. But the process is nice in that it keeps primary account numbers, credit card numbers, and personal information from traversing the network. It sends that token in its place. Digital rights management, or DRM is a suite of tools that is designed to limit how or where content can be accessed. That can be movies, music files, video files ort PDF documents. That was very big a while back, and it fell out of favor for a while, but there are new systems in place, and there's definitely a need to maintain some type of digital rights management to make sure that assets and products are not pirated or given to people that are not authorized to actually view them. It can prevent content from being copied, it can restrict what devices content can be viewed on, and it also may restrict how many times content can be accessed, say, for instance, on Netflix or one of the movie subscription services as an example. You can either rent a movie or you can buy the movie. If you rent it, you have access to it for a certain amount of time, and it's cheaper than actually buying it. But it's time based, so it may be for a day, a week, a month, however long, and then when that time is up, you can't access it anymore.

Chapter 4 Geographical Considerations & Cloud Access Security Broker

Another concept that I want you to be aware of is encryption. We talked about encryption before, but there's a couple things that I want to make sure you understand when we're talking about hardware-based encryption, encryption keys, and making sure that the information on our systems, whether it's a laptop, a desktop, server, those things can be secured properly. Two things I want to call to your attention. One is called a TPM, or a TPM chip, and that stands for a Trusted Platform Module. And a Trusted Platform Module, or a TPM chip, is a hardware chip that is embedded on a computer's motherboard, and it's used to store cryptographic keys that are used for encryption. We talked about encryption using public key, private key, or some type of encryption algorithm, whether it's symmetric or asymmetric. But those keys can be stored on the actual laptop, the motherboard itself. It's not an area you can access. It's not accessible to the user, but it is there to allow that cryptographic functionality in place. Something else is referred to as an HSM, or a hardware security Module. A hardware security Module is similar to a TPM, but HSMs are removable or external devices that can be added later. So both are used for encryption using RSA keys, and there are two different versions. One is a rack-mounted appliance. One is a card that would actually insert into a computer, a desktop or a server. Those things serve similar functionality but allow encryption of data on that device. When we're talking about architecting for security, there are some things around geographical considerations that you should be aware of as well, or should be in the back of your mind, at least. Where people log into can identify potential security issues. What do I mean by that? Well, logins from geographically diverse areas within a short period of time, unless, A, they're using a VPN and they're logging in from multiple locations in a very short period of time, like East Coast and then 10 minutes later, a half hour later, whatever, from the West Coast, that could be possible. There's really no reason to do that 9 times out of 10, that may raise a flag in and of itself. But logins from geographically diverse areas within a short period of time, so unless they're potentially magic or they've somehow defeated the laws of physics and can travel faster than the speed of light, then there is potentially a red flag. Those types of things should pop up. At least we should have some way of notifying or capturing those types of things and identifying, even better, alerting when those things happen. Also, foreign countries; if we're US based, as an example, and folks on our team always log in from somewhere within the US. They're not traveling abroad, but then all of a sudden there's a login from a foreign country. There should be mechanisms in place to log that and alert upon that, because that should be a red flag. Also unusual or flagged IP blocks. There are ranges of IP addresses that are known to be malicious, that are known to house spammers. Those types of things should also be logged and potentially blocked until it can be remediated or understood why this is happening. Next is something referred to as a cloud access security broker, so a CASB. What is it? Well, it helps control how we access cloud resources, so security policy enforcement points. We have on premise or in the cloud. This thing can be based in either location, and it's placed between the company, the consumer, and the cloud provider. It ensures that policies are enforced when accessing cloud-based assets. What policies are we talking about? Well, these are policies that are set by the company, not by the cloud provider, but our internal company. We may have our own methods, our own procedures, and our own standards for how things are accessed, our own security levels. This allows us to make sure those policies are enforced, such things as authentication, single sign-on, perhaps credential mapping, or even device profiling, and then, logging. All of these things, as a company, we want to make sure we have policies in place, and we can very easily make sure they're followed or enforced locally, within our own internal network. But now when we start accessing cloud-based resources we need to make sure that those policies are enforced as well. Along a similar line, we have something referred to as security as a service. Cloud providers can offer more security services cheaper, typically, or more effectively than on premise. Now that's not always the case. It depends upon the company, the size of your team, the level of expertise. But typically speaking, cloud providers operate on economies of scale, they have massive teams, typically, that have expertise in all of these areas. They can normally provide security as a service cheaper, they're more up to date, they have more resources, a deeper bench. Things like authentication, antivirus, anti-malware, antispyware, intrusion detection, they can offer pen testing services, or even SIEM services, security incident and event management services. It can offer all of these things as a cloud-based service, and it can operate strictly in the cloud, or it can also bridge into our internal networks as well. We can map authentication but we can also provide those services both in the cloud and on prem so that there's a bit of a blurring or no distinction between the functionality between those two environments. You may ask yourself, well, what's the difference between security as a service and a cloud access security broker? Well, we have cloud providers offer their services, infrastructure, resources to extend into a company's network. It's not just in the cloud; it's going to bridge into our network and blur that distinction between the two. They can provide those security services, typically at a cheaper TCO, or total cost of ownership, than the customer organization can. Again, not always across the board, depends upon the organization. Yours may be different. Whereas a cloud access security broker is going to sit between a customer's network and the cloud, and it acts as a broker or a services gateway. What it does is, enforce the customer organization's policies when accessing anything in the cloud. You can see there's a difference between the functionality between the two. Sometimes there is an overlap. Some security-as-a-service offerings may have a cloud access security-broker functionality built in, There is an overlap. But just understand the differences between those two. Can users recover their own passwords, and if so, ensure security questions aren't easily discoverable via social engineering? What do I mean by that? Social engineering can be very specific and can be very diabolical, in that someone can strike up a conversation with someone and in 5 minutes talk about their favorite dog, children's names, what their favorite car is, perhaps a favorite vacation spot, sports figure, just general conversation that seems like it's innocuous. But those things are typically, or at least a lot of times, what people will use as their password, or at least part of their password. It gives a social engineer, and a hacker, a bad actor, whatever you want to call them, it gives them a good starting point to try to guess passwords. If we don't train our users and we don't make them aware of these types of things, then more often than not, they don't know any better and they'll use these things as their password, easily guessable. So by policy, we can define if users need to call the help desk, or if they have a self-service mechanism in place to reset passwords. If they can do it themselves and make sure they're aware of some of the pitfalls and make sure it's complex enough that they can't reuse the same password over and over again or they can just increment it and say, , my favorite dog number 1, my favorite dog number 2. And then also our reuse policy, so they can't use the same two passwords back and forth month to month, back and forth. It just gives attackers and easy in into the network.

Chapter 5 Secure Protocols, SSL Inspection & Hashing

Next, let's talk about secure protocols, so SSL and TLS, two protocols that we should be aware of, Secure Sockets Layer and Transport Layer Security. These two things allow encryption or enable encryption when we're communicating between two hosts on a network. TLS is newer and it's based on SSL, and it also adds confidentiality and data integrity by encapsulating other protocols. We'll dig more into protocols itself later, but suffice it to say here that these are secure protocols that should be used whenever possible and also it initiates a stateful session with a handshake. It helps prevent eavesdropping and people jumping on the network and actually getting hold of that traffic. I mentioned before something called SSL and TLS inspection. That's an on-path type of an attack, formerly known as a man-in-the-middle attack. An SSL decryptor sits in between the user and the server. So both parties think they're connecting securely to each other, the host and also the server or the service that the host is connecting to. But they're actually both connecting to that SSL decryptor as an intermediary device. They're connecting there securely, but that device is acting as a man-in-the-middle or like on-path attack, although it's not really an attack per se because in this instance, it's actually owned by the corporation. It's just there to prevent someone from encrypting data and then sending it out of the network. They're checking it first to make sure that it meets policy. It inspects traffic to block sensitive information leakage, DLP, things like that, and also things like malware and ransomware, because that's becoming more and more common as well, where those things traverse over encrypted communication channels. Another concept I want to make sure you're familiar with is the concept of hashing. Hashing is a mathematical algorithm that's applied to a file before and also after transmission. If we hash a file, then we can tell if anything changes if we match those hashes before and after. If anything changes within the file, that hash will be completely different. There are a few types of hashing algorithms. We have MD5, SHA1, SHA2, and there's some others as well. But as an example, let's use SHA1, and we'll take a hash of a sentence. If you take a hash of that and if we change just one letter in that sentence, it's completely different. There's not even anything that's remotely the same between those two hashes. We can do that before we send something, and we can match it with how it was received on the other end. If those hashes are different in any way, shape, or form, we know that something happened. Either the data got corrupted or it was intercepted. Someone could have perhaps intercepted it, injected it with their own information, and put it back on the network and sent it to its host. These types of things allow us to verify the integrity of what we're sending. They can also be used when you're downloading something from the internet. If you go to a website and they say, here's our MD5 hash or our SHA1 hash or here is the hash. We'll let you download that file, you can run the same hash algorithm against that file, and if they don't match, well, then that you're downloading something that's not the same as what is advertised. Perhaps, again, it was corrupted or it was messed with in transit. So use that as a way to verify what you downloaded.

Chapter 6 API Gateways & Recovery Sites

From an architecture standpoint just some considerations, security vulnerabilities such as authentication, SQL injection, distributed denial-of-service attacks, and also portability between formats. Along those same lines there is something referred to as an API gateway. An API gateway can perform load balancing. It can also perform virus scanning, orchestration, authentication, data conversion, and more. Some of the things that I just talked about can be handled by an API gateway. As an example, let's say we have some back-end services, applications, data, services, and messaging, as an example, this group of back-end services, and then we have some customers that want to consume these services, mobile users, wearable users, smartphones, laptops. Well, we need some type of gateway that sits in between those two. And what's the purpose of an API? To put it very simply, if we're driving a car, we know how to drive pretty much any car out there unless it's something really funky. But generally speaking, you can pop into any car and how to drive it because how to operate the steering wheel. how to operate the gas pedal and the brake and the gear shift. You can think of that steering wheel, brake pedal, gas pedal as the API to the engine of the car. You don't have to know all the inner workings of the engine. You don't necessarily have to know it gets gasoline, does it have a carburetor, is it fuel injected, how many cylinders, any of that information. It doesn't matter which card you get into, it'll have an API, that's the same between different models of car. If we have an API that provides different functionality, the end user doesn't necessarily have to know what happens under the hood. We can change that without them even knowing it. All they have to know how to do is interact with the API. As you can see, the gateway acts as the intermediary piece. It provides that connectivity between the services on the back end and the API to the customer That all they have to understand is how does the API function. They don't need to know anything about the services on the back end. Now let's talk about recovery site options. What I mean when I say recovery site, we have a data center in location A. We need another data center that we can fail over to where we can recover to in the event of some type of disaster. Let's take a look at a few types of recovery sites and see the pros and cons. What's known as a cold site is really an empty building. This is somewhere we can fail over to. We're still going to bring in all of our equipment. We're going to have to move everything over, but at least we have a physical location. The pros, it's very inexpensive because it's just an empty shell, just a building that we have to move everything into. The cons, as you can imagine, long recovery time, could be weeks or even months depending upon the size of the organization, how much infrastructure you have to move. Additionally, all data is lost since your last backup, and do you have the money quickly available to purchase new equipment and/or services to make that move actually happen? Next we have a warm site. That's relatively inexpensive, but you can see the trend here. We have a cold, warm, and then we have hot, which we'll talk about in a moment. But a warm site is relatively inexpensive, but cheaper than a hot site. Some equipment is there, like phone, maybe the networks, but it's not ready for an immediate switchover. Recovery time could be a few days to a few weeks, again, depending upon the infrastructure, size of the company. But at least we have the bare bones are there. Next, we have a hot site. Pros, very quick to fail over and as you can imagine, a hot site is the most expensive of the three options. Infrastructure, replication, all these things that we have set up or want to have set up will come into play as far as determining cost. But just understand that out of the three, this is the most expensive. Duplicate infrastructure must be acquired and maintained. We would more than likely want to make sure that the equipment that is actually there is up to date, is patched, firmware. Replication, costs money. The amount of data that we want to replicate, we may need to have duplicate of everything. And then also bandwidth and location constraints may be in place, so synchronous failover or replication. If we're too far apart, if our data centers are too far away electronically, then that synchronous replication may not be there because of latency. And then, lastly, we have cloud based. Cloud based is more or less like DR as a Service or Disaster Recovery as a Service or cloud DR. It's managed by a provider typically. It's not managed by us. We go with an Amazon or Azure or xBase or Google or whoever your cloud provider of choice may be, it's managed by that provider. They have unlimited backup capacity as far as you're concerned. There's always a limit, but that's on their side. That's for them to worry about. As far as you're concerned, if you pay for it, you have endless backup capacity. Recovery times may be slower. Again, we're going now over the internet to a cloud-based provider. It's not local. It's not on-prem speeds. Another con, there may be confusion around types or best practices. What needs to be on prem? What needs to be off prem? Should we do a hybrid model, a multi-cloud model? But assuming those things are fleshed out, it is a good option, especially for companies that don't need or want to have a lot of extra equipment on site. When we're talking about DR failing over, let's say we have a data center here in Florida, somewhere in Central Florida. Not necessarily the best location as far as hurricane protection is concerned, but not a bad choice overall. So here we have our main data center. We also have a data center in Atlanta, Georgia. Geographically dispersed. We are in separate power grids. However, let's say, for instance, that hurricane that I mentioned just a moment ago starts to come up off the coast of Southern Florida. That potential is there for it to be in the same hurricane path or the path of that hurricane rather taking out both data centers if it were a large enough hurricane. The likelihood is small, but just some things to consider. When we're planning our data center locations, make sure that they're geographically dispersed enough That they can weather these types of storms, these type of events, so power grades, fuel availability, blast radius if it were some type of disaster or terrorist attack. A better option may be to move that data center far enough apart so that they're not in the same type of natural disaster type of zone. If we need synchronous replication, they have to be close enough electronically so we have very, very low latency, round trip time between the sites. If that's not an issue, you could even move it anywhere else within the country so it acts more as a failover bunker, a data ring bunker. It's going to be asynchronous replication because we're too far apart electronically to really have that low latency that we may need for certain applications. Databases, as an example, are typically very latency-dependent or latency-sensitive. But if that's not an issue for you, perhaps you have West Coast customers and East Coast customers, and all you need to do is make sure the data is available in the event of a disaster and doesn't need to be real time, this could be a great option as well.

Chapter 7 Honeypots, Fake Telemetry & DNS Sinkhole

The next concept is something referred to as a honeypot. As the old saying goes, you can catch more flies with honey than you can with vinegar, and the same thing holds true here when we're talking about looking for bad actors. A honeypot is a computer or host that's set up to specifically become a target of attack. We're making it very attractive to bad actors. We want to provide them with a landing spot, somewhere to come in and try to hack through that we're monitoring and keeping a close eye on. That way we can identify the tactics, techniques, and procedures that they're using and potentially even reverse-engineer some of what they're doing. The basics of a honeypot, we want to have it appear to have sensitive information. We also want to make sure that it's monitored, and we want to identify hackers, learn their methods and also their techniques, and then we have something along the same lines referred to as honeyfiles. It's similar in concept, but it applies to individual files versus an actual system, but it's still the same net result. It's designed to entice bad actors and to monitor their activities. Next, we have a honeynet, so similar to a honeypot, but larger in scale. A network setup that's intentionally designed for attack so that the attackers can be monitored and also studied. In this example, we have a network setup that looks very similar to a normal production network. We'll have a publicly-facing infrastructure that the hacker or bad actor would potentially come through. They'll hit our switches. We have management servers set up. We might have a honeywall, which is a firewall designed and specifically monitored with vulnerabilities in mind to allow hackers to come through. They think, ooh, I'm getting something special here. They bust through that firewall or that honeywall, and then they have access to the network that we've set up. And we may have infrastructure that is reflective of a normal production network, Linux hosts, Windows hosts. And at that point we sit back and watch what they do, understand their techniques, follow them through the network, see what they're trying to potentially get to, and it gives us clues as to how they operate and potentially even allow us to trace back to the actual location of those bad actors. Telemetry information is all of the ancillary information that's provided or created by something like, say, for instance, a Tesla car. There's tons and tons of telemetry data, all the different things around that system, electricity consumption, wear and tear on the individual components, speed, so on and so on. All of those things get fed back constantly to corporate, and then they use that data, they mine that data, and then develop patches, understand how things operate. Those types of things happen with everything, cable boxes, cell phones, I mean you name it. Everything generates telemetry data. Well, by generating fake telemetry data, we can have applications that can pretend to be useful utilities when in actuality, they're not. As an example, an anti-virus and anti-malware fake. Those things will actually pop up and claim to find fake viruses or malware. They may show report data that looks very, very convincing. And then what happens, it tricks the user into paying for premium support, i.e. virus removal. It can also install additional malware behind the scenes and actually make things worse. But these applications that are providing that fake telemetry look very, very convincing to the end user if they don't know any better. This is where training and conversations come into play, making sure that people look out for these types of things They don't fall victim. Next we have something referred to as a DNS sinkhole. A DNS sinkhole is a DNS server that supplies false results. You may think, well, that's no good. Well, it can be used constructively or maliciously. It doesn't necessarily have to be a bad thing. Although it sounds like a bad thing at first, it's not necessarily. In most cases, it's not. Example use cases, a DNS server that's operating as a DNS sinkhole can be used for good purposes, as an example, deploying a DNS sinkhole high up in the DNS hierarchy to stop a botnet from operating across the internet. And in a lot of instances, this is how they do that. The botnets that are set up and operate at large, large scales across the internet with thousands of hosts, all of those hosts will typically hit DNS for a domain name, and then they'll respond back to that domain name. Well, if we use a DNS sinkhole, that provides false results, so when that DNS query gets sent, instead of going to the proper host, we actually send it to a another host, that can effectively shut down that botnet or at least for a period of time. In a malicious instance, actors can use a DNS sinkhole along the same lines to redirect users to a malicious website. A user thinks they're visiting CNN as an example, when they think they're actually visiting the correct site. If a DNS sinkhole is in place and they're redirected to a false or malicious website, it may look like the actual website they're trying to visit, but it's obviously not the right one. But when they put in their username, credentials, even though it fails and the user thinks there's a problem with the website, what happens is the bad actor captures those credentials and then can use them for malicious purposes. In summary we talked about security concepts in an enterprise environment. We talked about configuration management, data sovereignty. We talked about data protection, some geographical considerations, along with site resiliency and also some things around deception and disruption with honeyfiles, honeynets and DNS sinkholes.

Chapter 8 Cloud Storage and Cloud Computing

In the following chapters, we'll be covering understanding virtualization and also cloud computing. We'll be talking about cloud models, we'll talk about managed service providers, and we'll also talk about the concept of fog and also edge computing, two new terms you may or may not be familiar with. We'll talk about microservices and APIs or application programming interfaces. We'll also talk about SDN and SDV, software-defined networking and software-defined visibility. We'll talk about serverless architecture and also virtualization. What is the cloud? Well, the cloud is one of those buzzwords, , quote unquote, that everyone is talking about right now, whether it be security professionals and they're talking about the cloud, or application developers need to make their applications cloud ready, or whatever the case might be, everyone is talking about the cloud. Well, the cloud, in a very basic sense, is storage that's external to a company's data center. So you're storing stuff outside of your own data center. It's accessible from the outside world, whether it be publicly accessible to everyone or only people with proper credentials, it depends upon the application, and then you also need to define is it simply storage, or is there automation behind that? In other words, is it just an application that is cloud-enabled, it sits out in some public data center, or is it something that you may offer to your internal customers and give them the ability to provision virtual machines, to provision databases, to provision some type of development environment, whether it might be OpenShift or Cloud Foundry or some type of development environment to allow them to quickly spin up that environment. That all can focus around a cloud infrastructure. And then, as we talked about before, there are different types of clouds. There are public clouds, private clouds, and then a hybrid combination thereof. Cloud, when it refers to a security posture, we need to just understand, really, are there policies in place, are there access controls, as to who can access that data? We need to make sure that we audit third-party providers to ensure that their security practices are at least as stringent as our own. Because remember, we talked about previously, our security, just generally speaking, is really only as effective as the weakest link. So only the strongest is the weakest link. That pretty much goes for anything, but it's especially important with security. It doesn't matter if we have millions of dollars in locks and controls, if on the side, attached to our network, is a third-party hosting provider, and they have abysmal security. Someone could walk right in through the side door and get into our company's network. That doesn't do us much good. We need to make sure that all of these things are lockstep with each other so that we have a consistent security posture. Something else to keep in mind, is the data copied to multiple data centers? When they replicate, most times, they're going to replicate that data to three or more data centers. Is it within the same geographic region, or do they copy that off-site somewhere, or do they copy that out of the country? It's important to understand where that data is being copied to and replicated to from a compliance perspective, but also from a security perspective. As we talk about the evolution of virtualization, cloud computing is really the next step. Cloud computing is the virtualization of infrastructure, platform, and services, and it really just depends upon what level of virtualization and what level of services are being offered to the end user. In a nutshell, it gives us automation and self-service. In a cloud platform, or a cloud environment, depending upon whether it's infrastructure, platform, or software, there is a level of automation and self-service. A user can go in and perhaps provision their own virtual machines, or provision their own databases, or they may be able to provision their own development environment, test their applications, spin up some type of test dev environment. Or they may just go in and just start using an application. It just really depends upon what platform we're virtualizing. It's a reduced time to market, and it also gives us an increased speed to develop our applications and deliver value to the business. Cloud computing is made up of a couple different services. We have infrastructure-as-a-service, or IaaS, platform-as-a-service, or PaaS, and then software-as-a-service, or SaaS. And there are a couple different variations of cloud computing. We have a private cloud, we have a public cloud, a hybrid, and then community. I'll talk about each of these in a little more detail in just a moment. Collectively, though, that's called the cloud. That is just what the cloud is. And it means different things to different people, but in a nutshell, it is a virtualized infrastructure that provides some level of service, and it gives it in an automated fashion. Let's go ahead and talk about X-as-a-Service. When I say X-as-a-Service, what do I mean by that? Well you can insert the buzzword, It means everything these days is turned into a service, as the flavor of the day. It is virtualization and commoditization of almost every layer of the IT "stack". It provides for quicker deployment along with increased HA and DR, HA being high availability and DR being disaster recovery. When I talk about these X-as-a-Service, I'm talking about infrastructure, platform, network, storage, compute, security; you name it, these different verticals are now being turned into a service.

Chapter 9 IaaS, PaaS & SaaS

As an example, let's look at Infrastructure as a Service. Infrastructure as a Service, or IaaS, allows for the distribution and consumption of resources as a service as the name implies. So multiple users can utilize the same infrastructure, hence it's a multi-tenant environment, meaning we can have multiple customers all using that same infrastructure, and it allows you to fully utilize that infrastructure because as some people are using it fully, others are not, and vice versa, so that way the infrastructure itself doesn't sit idle very long. It also allows for elastic scaling as needs and demands increase and decrease. You don't necessarily have to spin up a very large environment at first, you can spin up a small environment, have everything you need for an initial deployment, and then as things start to ramp up, as it becomes more popular, or as let's say for instance you start advertising in certain markets or for whatever reason those things start to speed up and the actual interest starts to heat up and now the service is becoming popular, you can increase dynamically the resources allocated to that service, and then when those things die down, those resources can be destroyed or taken down, leaving you with just what you need. So it allows you to pay for what you need as you go, rather than having to invest a lot in infrastructure right up front. What it does, it prices things as a utility model. It shifts the spend from CAPEX, or capital expenditures, to OPEX, operating expense. It turns it almost into a utility bill. These types of things can also either be private or public or both, you can have a hybrid model. These things can be spun up, as I said, dynamically to adjust to a specific user's needs. Something else I want to make sure that we're clear on is the fact that IaaS lends itself or leverages automation and also self-service. That's one of the milestones of that type of platform. It enables a customer to select their own hardware and software configurations and then provision their own infrastructure. As an example, we have a user who would then access a self-service portal - some website that gives them some ability to pick and choose their configurations. And then from there, they'll typically have sizes that they can pick from, in this case, a small, medium, and a large. A small might have a server with a single CPU and a certain amount of RAM and storage. A medium configuration might have double the CPU and RAM and storage. And then the large might have three or four times that amount of CPU and RAM and storage. It allows for a standardized set of offerings, which makes it very easy to set up and configure, where you can have all your changes pre-approved in change management. These are known configurations, these are known reference architectures, but it gives the user some choice so they can have small, medium, large, or whatever a combination of choices you want to provide to them, but it gives them that option. They can quickly pick and choose. They don't have to worry about configuring and racking and stacking all the things that are typically associated with that infrastructure. They go to the portal, click a few buttons, and then within a few minutes or a couple hours or whatever the approval process is behind the scenes, that infrastructure is then made available to them. It lends itself very nicely to test dev environments or POC environments where we need to spin up some infrastructure to test out an idea, or to build some type of test lab. It ultimately speeds up the time to market considerably. Next, we have Platform-as-a-Service, or PaaS. PaaS environments comprise of computational resources, typically a test and dev environment, or DevOps environment, that can be easily created and configured. In a PaaS environment, you don't care about the infrastructure underlying it. You don't care about how the servers are spun up and how they're racked and stacked, and configured, and IP'd, and access controls, and all those types of things; all you want really in a PaaS environment is to deliver a development platform to your developers They can quickly do what developers do, which is develop applications, iterate through, and deliver some type of service. There's no need to order, acquire rack/stack hardware, configure the network IP addresses, stand up load balancers, VLANS, install software; all of these things are typically associated with an Infrastructure-as-a-Service, a PaaS or a Platform-as-a-Service sits on top of that. All of those things are beneath that layer. Then as you can imagine, test environments can very quickly be created, expanded as needed, and then you can run tests, you can report, and then tear those things down on demand. It allows for a very quick iterative process, and it lends itself very well to a DevOps model. Also, multi-tenant, where many users can use the same set of resources. we don't have to buy a lot of infrastructure, and only when we're using it do we get utility out of it, if we're not using it, someone else is. If we have a multi-tenant environment, we're ensuring that that infrastructure gets utilized much more fully. Just as an example of a few PaaS providers, we have AWS, or Amazon Web Services. They have one referred to as Elastic Beanstalk, Windows Azure or Azure, depending upon who you talk to, Heroku, Force.com, and I'll go through the rest of these or you can read through the rest of these rather. They're all providing some type of Platform-as-a-Service. Some are more mature than others, and I'm not really recommending one over the other. However, we know which one is really the 900 pound gorilla in the room, but there are others and they all provide similar types of services. Next we have SaaS, or Software as a Service, and as you might guess, it's now Software as a Service, meaning we don't have to go out and buy a specific software, we don't have to turn around and install it on our individual servers, Applications that can be provided on demand. No setup, no installation, no configuration required. Much easier than buying, , 300 copies of something and going around in the old days and either sneaker-netting, , installing those things on individual workstations, or putting it on a network share and having people install, or some automated method where we're pushing it out, maybe via group policy or some type of packaging mechanism; Software as a Service, none of that is really necessary. You sign up for it, and we can either access it as a web portal or a web service, or it may download and install on our workstation. Examples might be Salesforce, Office 365, and Google Apps, those are three big ones, there's obviously lots and lots out there, but you get the general idea of what Software as a Service is and how that can make an environment much more agile. From a security perspective, these things work well; however, just understand you may or may not have control over the security that takes place with some of these types of Software as a Service providers, depending upon the agreement you have in place, depending upon where that actual software resides. Just to point out the differences between IaaS, PaaS and SaaS, we have Infrastructure-as-a-Service, you manage from the OS up, and you can see the distinction, networking, storage, servers, and virtualization, that's all managed by the vendor. You manage OS, middleware, runtime, data, and applications, That manages up the stack. Platform-as-a-Service you would manage from the data layer up. You manage the applications and the data. You don't care about the runtime, the middleware, the OS, the virtualization, the racking, stacking, configuring all of those things, you don't care about that. All you want is that Platform-as a-Service or that development environment; and then Software-as-a-Service, you manage nothing. You can see everything is provided by the vendor. Something to keep in mind if you're running a private cloud, then you are the vendor, and the customers, or your customers, are the actual managers, So depending upon where you sit in this scenario will depend upon whether you're the vendor or the manager.

Chapter 10 Managed Service Providers, Fog Computing & Edge Computing

Just to call your attention to the different types of clouds we talked about briefly before, we have a private cloud, and in a private cloud, you manage and maintain all resources. It could be IaaS, PaaS, or SaaS. Then we have a public cloud. A cloud provider manages those resources. That's going to be a hosted platform typically. You control the data, they control the actual infrastructure. Then we have a hybrid model, where we have a public and private mix. Typically, those things will start internally where a company will have a private cloud, and then as things grow, they might expand out into a public cloud, which, allows them that elastic growth where they can expand and contract as necessary. Then we have a community cloud. So, resources are shared among several groups or organizations. They may not necessarily be in the same company, but they may have common goals. Oftentimes companies will group resources so they have access to the same applications. That can be public or private, but costs for that specific cloud are spread across the members of the cloud. Next, let's talk about managed service providers, or MSPs. We mentioned them previously, but just to recap, an MSP, or managed service provider, delivers services either on-prem or at a customer's site, in the MSP's data center, or in a third-party data center, and typically, a managed service provider will provide the following things: they'll do network, application, infrastructure, and then also security. They don't necessarily have to provide all of these things, but they certainly can. When you switch over to a managed service provider, they'll either come in on-prem and manage your infrastructure, manage stuff in your data center, or, you can put it in their data center or a third party. You can think of it as outsourcing your IT department. They're going to take care of application, network, infrastructure, security, storage, compute, all of these things, or a combination thereof. Conversely, a managed security service provider, or an MSSP, they're going to do things around, obviously, security. MSPs provide outsourced monitoring and management of security devices and systems, usually in a 24x7 fashion. Again, you can think of it as outsourcing a piece or the entirety of your IT department. In this case, we're doing security. Things like firewalls, intrusion detection, virtual private networks, or VPNs, also vulnerability scans, anti-virus, antimalware, and ransomware protection, things along those lines. A lot, if not all of these things, can be outsourced and handled by a third party. There is some differences between on-prem versus off-prem, obviously. In an on-prem environment, you own the infrastructure. Whether you buy it as a capital expenditure or you're leasing it, you still, for all intents and purposes, own that infrastructure. It's your equipment. But along those same lines, you also have more control on customization and non-standard builds, so you're not relegated to just the sizes that a managed service provider or someone outsourcing may provide to you. If it's your equipment, your IT department, your everything, then you can build it however you want. That's not necessarily a good thing. We talked before about standardization and how that actually improves things like security, eliminates risk, makes administration easier, but there are instances where you may need to have a custom type of build, and this will allow for that. Also, you have more direct control over policies, management, and administration, as I just talked about. On the downside, you also have a continual upgrade and a continual refresh of that infrastructure. Typically, it's a three year or a five year cycle where you're going to swap out that infrastructure. Depending upon what it is you're replacing, it can be a pretty monumental effort, especially for a large storage array or maybe your SAN infrastructure. Things that have a lot of tie-ins and a lot of dependencies, it's much more of a task to coordinate all of these different teams and make sure that that migration goes smoothly. And then also, depending upon how your company is structured and what you have tolerance for, when you buy your own equipment, it's typically a capital expenditure, or a CAPEX expenditure. Some companies like that, some do not, it just depends upon the individual company. When we're talking about off-prem, you don't own the equipment, it's managed by the provider. Having said that, you have less control over customization, policies, and overall administration, which again may or may not be a big deal to you, depending upon what it is you want to do with that infrastructure. On the upside, there's no lifecycle or maintenance activities, That's a big one. You don't have to worry about constantly refreshing that infrastructure. You don't have to worry about patching and security. That's managed by the provider as well. Lifecycle activities, patching, security updates, anti-virus, antimalware, they actually manage. Then it's also an operating expense, or OPEX, versus CAPEX, and that's good in the fact that you don't necessarily have to buy everything up front. You don't have to buy hundreds of computers or thousands of computers, large storage arrays, SAN infrastructure, and front-load all of that expense. When you buy that in a CAPEX model, you can pay for just what you consume. When you're buying it in a third-party or an off-prem situation, you're not buying the entire storage array. You're only buying what you need. You're not buying hundreds of servers or thousands of servers. You're buying as much as you need. If it's Azure, Amazon, Google, a lot of the bigger cloud providers, they have a very mature elastic capability, so as you grow, or as you need to grow, you can grow dynamically, and then when you don't need all of that infrastructure, it can be collapsed or destroyed That you only are paying for what you need at that point in time. The next term I want to talk about is something referred to as fog computing. Fog computing, along the same lines where we're keeping the theme of the cloud, well, fog computing extends cloud computing to the network edge. It takes the cloud and it makes it a foggy bridge into the local, or at least a part of the local network, or the edge of your individual network. Edge computing we'll talk about more in just a moment as well, but with edge computing we're processing data local to where it was created, That's a subset of fog computing, so keep that in mind. Edge computing we'll talk about in a moment. That's a subset of the overall bigger picture of fog computing. Fog computing is comprised of compute, network, and storage that bridges the gap between everything being in the cloud and then also some stuff on-prem or at the edge of the customer's premise. We take a look at this in more detail. We have the edge, and in the edge environment we may have things like IoT devices, applications, telemetry, information. Those things feed edge networks and they need local low-latency processing, It doesn't make sense to send all of that data all the way back to some central processing area, in the cloud to be processed, analyzed, and then perhaps fed back to the local devices that generated that to make decisions or have some type of interaction with that device. It's a lot of back and forth traffic that's unnecessary. By having things at the edge, all of these devices, they feed into a local or an edge network that can process that in a much more expedited fashion, low latency. In between, we have the fog network, or the fog layer. That's distributing compute, storage, and networking, again, closer to users for real-time processing. We have a bunch of servers and networking, and there's some storage intermixed in there as well. That bridges between the cloud and the edge. It gives us that distributed compute, storage, and networking for things that really require that real-time processing or low-latency applications. Then we have the cloud. The cloud you can think of as a very deep, very large lake that everything can be dumped into. It's great for deep data analytics and processing, also long-term storage and archiving, things like massive parallel data processing, things where we need a very large amount of compute, network, storage, big data mining, machine learning, all of these things lend themselves very well to the cloud, but not the fastest thing out there, and it doesn't actually interact with things on the edge as quickly as it could. So having things in the cloud is great for large scale, then we have an intermediate layer, which is the fog layer. That's going to be for things that are really high speed, low latency, real-time processing. Then down at the edge, that's more or less on the customer's prem, and that's bleeding into their network, so the fog will connect those two layers together. Next we have edge computing, and edge, is sometimes interchanged with fog computing. Edge and fog are sometimes interchangeable, but they're not necessarily the same thing. Edge computing puts resources close to where the data is created, and it's a subset of fog computing. Storage, compute, and network close to the edge. It is a part of it or it works in tandem with fog computing, but as we saw, it's a separate layer. The fog computing layer bridges that gap between the cloud and the edge.

Chapter 11 VDI, Virtualization & Containers

Virtual Desktop Infrastructure, or VDI and VDI provides for centralized hosting of management and desktop images. Users access their desktop from the server. A user will access their actual desktop not on their local PC or their laptop, they will in essence terminal server in to the server, the VDI server, and they will be presented with their desktop image at that point. We have a centralized virtual desktop infrastructure of a VMware vSphere server cluster. We have some link clones, they're going to be our parent image, and we have a golden image, that is, this is what we're giving to either all of our users or we're going to give one image for our developers, one image for our finance folks, one image for our call center; and then we have linked clones that have different sets of applications that are fed on top of that parent image, and then we have some type of presentation server. When that user connects to that desktop, they're either going to have persistent desktops so they can install things, they can install their own software, make their own configuration changes in the look and feel. Or it could be a non-persistent desktop, so when they log off, everything goes back to its original pristine state. The next time they log in, it looks just like it did before. But the benefits of a VDI infrastructure as you might imagine, is the fact that we can manage everything centrally. We can patch all of our desktops in one location, we can make sure that they're all identical, so they can start off with a non-persistent fashion, so every time they log in they get exactly the same desktop. We can create different policies for different groups, so that certain groups, developers, finance, or they'll get different images, but they're all the same as far as within that individual group. It makes it much easier to manage. The only thing they really need to have on their end is a lower-end terminal. They don't necessarily have to have a high-end PC. They can really have a dumb terminal, for that matter, that has no hard drive or so forth. It just has a connection to the Internet or Ethernet jack rather, out to either the local network or the Internet, and as soon as they connect to that presentation server, they're presented with a full-blown desktop. It just makes things easier from the life of an administrative perspective, also from a security perspective. There are some challenges sometimes around bandwidth and connectivity. If the connectivity between the end user and that presentation server is down or congested, then they're going to have some difficulty actually doing anything, it may halt their productivity for a period of time until that's corrected, but the benefits far outweigh the negatives. As far as terminal services go, and VDI is really a component of that, we have two different things to keep in mind here as well. We have terminal services and then we have application delivery services. If we break those into two separate entities, we have application streaming, and here we have an application streaming server. We'll have an operating system, we have app 1, 2, 3, as you might see, and those apps can individually be pushed down to the clients. They run in a virtualized container on that client. Each client has their own full-blown operating system, their full-blown PC or laptop, but the applications that run on top of that laptop or that PC are virtualized containers that are pushed out from the application streaming server. Microsoft's App-V is an example of that. We also have terminal services, which you may or may not be familiar with. Terminal services, everything runs on the server and it's simply displayed to the host. We can have a terminal server that users will use either RDP or Citrix ICA Client, or some type of remote desktop tool. They'll log into that presentation server, everything actually happens on the server, and the only thing that gets sent to the client are graphic updates, when things change on the screen, mouse clicks, keyboard presses. All they really see is the graphical representation of what's taking place on the server. We have the benefit of being able to patch everything from one central location, we can control everything from a centralized location, whether it's a single server or a server farm, we can patch everything at once, It gives us the opportunity to have things in a more secure, a more locked down environment. It depends upon connectivity, bandwidth. You may or may not have connectivity issues or challenges, but if people are working remotely, say from across the state, across the country, or perhaps even globally, if that connectivity is not there, you can halt their productivity until that comes back. So just some things to keep in mind there, but from a security perspective it offers a lot of advantages. The next concept is virtualization, and virtualization is really a big jump forward, in the last 10 years or so we've been able to virtualize pretty much everything. It started off with virtualizing workstations, this moved onto servers and storage, and then networking. All of the main areas within a typical IT department, with a typical IT infrastructure, have now been able to be virtualized, and there's a number of major players in that space that you should just be aware of. I'm not endorsing one over the other, but VMware, Microsoft Hyper-V, KVM, and Oracle all have their own virtualization platforms, and what virtualization really does, it takes the capabilities and the personality of a physical device and it converts it to a virtual representation. Meaning we can take a PC or a server, all the physical attributes, all the things that you typically associate with that server, the amount of CPU capability, the processor, the network, the amount of RAM and so on; we can virtualize that and place it into a container, if you will, onto another server. In other words, we could take 5, 10, 15, 20 physical servers, virtualize those, and put those virtual representations or those virtual containers onto a single server, in this instance, let's just say like a VMware ESX cluster. We could take a number of servers, put them onto one physical box. That's going to allow us to perform the same functions as the physical counterpart. It will lower our infrastructure costs because instead of having to buy 20 or 30 servers now, we can simply buy 20 or 30 licenses and put them on a single physical server or a cluster. So, we're going to lower infrastructure costs; however, you'll notice that we're going to increase licensing costs, the hypervisor license for those individual VMs. In a traditional server, we have the server at the bottom. We install an operating system on top of that server, and then we install our applications on top of the operating system. That's just a typical server rollout or a typical workstation. In a VMware or a virtualized environment, it works the same amongst all of the virtualization platforms. We have our server or our cluster of servers, we're going to lay the hypervisor on top, in this case, in this example it's VMware, and then on top of that, we're going to lay down individual VMs, and each of the guests are comprised of an OS and an app or multiple apps. We're in essence, taking what used to be a physical server, virtualizing that into a single container, and dropping that on top of our hypervisor. In this VMware example, we have an ESX cluster, you'll notice four servers in our cluster. We have our VMware OS on top of that, it's a virtual symmetric multi-processing operating system. We have in this example four VMs sitting on top of that. We have one with four cores, one with one, two, and then one. Each one of our VMS are individual, they're distinct entities just as if they were physical servers and they can have their own number of processors, their own amount of memory, own amount of storage and so on; and we can dynamically dial that up or down. If we find that we have a VM that's not really performing as well as it should, we can actually add more processors or more processing power, or more memory to that VM, dynamically. In some instances, depending upon the software, it might require a reboot, but regardless, we can add resources to that rather than having to go out and buy a new physical server. On the ESX cluster itself or the ESX host, we have a pooled or a set of pooled resources. CPU, memory, storage, and network, all of that is shared among all of the VMs sitting on that ESX cluster. Instead of having a physical server for every application, let's say we have five databases, instead of having five physical servers like we would do in a traditional environment, we can have one ESX cluster and then five VMS. That way each of the VMs are much more fully utilized, and the actual EXS cluster, the physical hardware, is much better utilized. We also reduce power, cooling, heating and cooling and so on. There are a few different types of, or categories of servers, virtualized servers, that we should be aware of. First is Type I. A Type I virtualized server runs on bare metal, it's a bare-metal server. And guests run on that host, which is the actual ESX, in this case the VMware ESX server, that's going to run on a bare-metal server. In other words, there's no operating system underneath of that. The VMware ESX server has his own operating system, so that gets loaded onto that bare-metal host. That host can then run individual guest operating systems. That individual guest can be Windows or Linux or some other variation, it doesn't have to necessarily be just the same type of OS that the ESX server itself is. The ESX server, in other words, might be a Linux installation or a Linux flavor under the hood. However, it could run Linux, Windows on top. Each of those is its own virtual server. It's got its own operating system, its own drivers, its own binaries, and applications. It gets a virtual NIC, or network interface card, it gets its own IP address, so for all intents and purposes, it is a separate server. It appears to the outside world as a separate, distinct entity. A Type II server runs on top of an OS. It runs on top of the OS, which runs on top of the bare-metal box, the bare-metal server. The host runs on top of an operating system, Windows or Linux, and then the guests run inside of that host. We have VMware Workstation or a Virtual Box, Oracle's Virtual Box are good examples of this. The guests run at a third layer above the hardware. In the first example, we had those guests running at the second layer above the hardware. In this instance, they run at the third layer above the hardware. We have a bare-metal server, we have our Windows or Linux operating system, and then we have VMware Workstation or Oracle Virtual Box or some other type of virtualization software running, and then inside of that we have our individual operating systems, They're distinct operating systems within that Type II virtualized infrastructure. And then to contrast that we have something referred to as container-based or containers. That is an operating system virtualization. It's very lightweight. These containers can start up in milliseconds, whereas typically, just as you would imagine with a server when it boots up and has to load the BIOS or the UEFI interface, it has to load the drivers. Then it loads the actual operating system, and then all the applications, and then the drivers inside of that. It can sometimes take 10 to 15 seconds or more up to 30 seconds or a minute, depending on how old your system is, for that operating system in that server to fully boot. Well, in a container-based world, those things can spin up extremely fast. They're very lightweight, and they can start up in milliseconds. It's a little bit different approach than we saw in Type I and Type II. We have our bare-metal server, we have our operating system, and then on top of that are containers. Those containers only really have the application and the binaries. Those data boxes contain the libraries and the binaries that the applications need to run. It's not a full-blown operating system. You can spin up containers, if you will. These containers, these little micro segments of the things that are needed for that application, they can spin up very quickly. They can expand as needed to provide additional resources, they can contract just as quickly when those resources are not necessary. It allows you to elastically expand out and provide infrastructure, provide services when the demand gets high, and then it contracts when it's not needed. In the VMware, you'll see we have our host OS, which sits on top of the server. There's a hypervisor then that sits on top of that. From there, we have our guest OS, our binaries and libraries, and then application, Application A. Then we have a separate guest that has its guest operating system, binaries, libraries, and then Application B. We can have multiple guests running on that host, or that VMware ESX server. In the container example we have our server and our host OS, and then on top of that we have something referred to as a Docker Engine in this container example. From there, we have Application A, Application B, C, and so on, each of which only contain the binaries and the libraries necessary for that application. You can deploy very lightweight, you don't have to worry about patching all the things that a typical operating system would need to be patched, and virus updates. It's only the things that are specific to that application. It allows you to expand very quickly, and those containers can also run on any operating system or any platform that has that Docker engine. You provide the binaries and libraries for that application, but it allows you to deploy to pretty much any type of infrastructure that hosts a Docker-like container system. Its very scalable, and it can contract just as quickly. From a security perspective, the advantages of this would be you don't have to patch a bunch of different operating systems, you don't have to patch individual OS's and all of these containers, you're providing a bare minimum of what's necessary to run that application. But even to take a step back for our Type I and Type II's, it's an advantage in the fact that we can patch from a centralized location. We can go to our ESX server and patch all of the hosts on that server relatively quickly - same thing if we start to have a resource contention or we understand that things are starting to slow down on a specific ESX host, we can migrate that data and those workloads. We can migrate those VMs from one ESX server to another, it's called vMotioning, and in doing so, we can free up resources on the ESX server that's exhibiting contention. It gives us the ability to scale when necessary, we can move things over. If we need to patch the actual ESX host itself, we can migrate the workloads off to another ESX server. We can then bring that ESX server down, patch it, upgrade it, do what we need to do, and then once it comes back up, we can migrate or vMotion those VMs back over again, It gives us a very convenient way to patch our systems with minimum downtime. The takeaway here, however, is to understand what is a Type I, Type II, and container-based virtualization, and the general benefits and disadvantages, as far as security is concerned, from each of these platforms.

Chapter 12 Microservices and APIs

With microservices what we're doing is taking an application and breaking it apart into individual functions. Microservices treats each function of an application as an independent service that can be altered, updated, taken down without affecting the rest of the application. It's easily maintained. Each function or each service, or microservice, is loosely coupled and extensible, It can be changed, added, increased or tweaked in some fashion without affecting the other components, and it's also independently deployable. If we look at this in a little more detail, typically considered legacy, we have what's called a monolithic architecture, and in there we had a user interface, business logic, a data interface, maybe a backend database. If we wanted to add features or functionality or change anything on that application, we had to change everything - the entire application, because it was treated as one monolithic thing. With microservices, on the other hand, we have a microservices architecture that breaks all of that apart. All of the individual main functions, business logic, data interface, all of those things now become microservices, and each of those can be developed independently, they can be deployed independently, and they can scale independently. They all talk to one another in some fashion. One can be pulled out or updated and then redeployed without affecting the rest of the application, It allows for very quick and easy updating, and also it allows the application to scale very easily. If we look at this in more detail, let's say, for instance, we have a mobile app, and then we have an API gateway, an application programming interface. Normally, that's how we'll interact with a microservice in some fashion. The mobile app may connect to that API gateway via a REST API. Conversely, we have a web browser. It's going to connect to a storefront, which is a web application. Again, it will do that over the web. Well, on the backend, via REST APIs, we're connecting to different services, different microservices, which then connect to databases on the backend. Whether we come in via a mobile app or a web browser, we're still typically interacting via some type of

API between where we're at and the information that we're interacting with on the backend. Whether we come in through a mobile app, and we're doing it through a REST API, or we're coming in through a web browser through some type of web frontend, once it hits the backend and starts to go into the account services and the microservices and all the infrastructure behind, there's APIs in place that allow all of these things to connect and talk to each other, but they're also loosely coupled so that one can be pulled out, updated, tweaked, expanded or scaled or even reduced without affecting the rest. Some microservices key points, some things that I want to make sure that you take away from this, is the fact that applications are broken apart by function. No longer is it a monolithic app that has every single thing packaged together as one entity, we now break things apart. All services are created individually and deployed separately from one another. Next, each component is loosely coupled, so different groups even can develop different functions and different services. Not one group has to work on an application, it could be spread across, and each service can be changed or upgraded without affecting the others. It can even be scaled. It deployed via containers, typically, we have something like Kubernetes and Docker for orchestration, or some other type of orchestration engine, then each microservice is packaged as a container image, and then as we scale, it quickly scales because scaling is done based on the changing number of container instances. If we need more, we just spin up more containers so we can handle more load, and additionally, we can spin up or scale down each individual microservice. It doesn't have to be done across the board. If all we need is database processing or some type of interaction with maybe networking or a decision engine or a recommendation engine or whatever that service might be, that specific service can spin up independent of all the others.

Chapter 13 Infrastructure as Code (IAC) & Software Defined Networking (SDN)

Infrastructure as Code is a methodology to create repeatable processes for deploying infrastructure. What it does is it replaces static scripts, and the point is here, we're trying to move away from static scripts where everybody maintains their own repository of information of scripts and the way they do things, and more or less make it standardized and deployable across the enterprise, so code can be reused between groups. Collaboration and automation tools like Puppet, Chef, Ansible, there's a number of them out there, can speed delivery. It can make things faster, it can make things standardized across the environment, and it also reduces shadow IT, and it makes processes more secure and reduces the risk of human error. The more we can derisk the environment, the better off we are. Next, let's talk about SDN, or Software Defined Networking. What this does, much like we talked about with microservices, this decouples the management plane from the data plane. We're breaking things apart. It places intelligence higher up the stack. The switches that used to have all the intelligence in each individual switch or each individual router, now those things almost become dumb devices, and all of the intelligence is placed up at a controller at a higher level that can control all of the switches, all of the routers, all of your networking infrastructure as a single unit. It's a holistic view of the network, and programmatic tuning could take place based upon activity, on workloads. So, routers and switches, more or less become dumb devices with the intelligence handled by a centralized controller suite. We're simply moving that administration up the stack, Instead of having to go into each individual switch, each individual router and configure things, we can now do things up at a higher level and push those changes out to the entire network at once. Along those same lines is something referred to as Software-Defined Visibility, or SDV. What this is, is a "visibility fabric," in quotes, that can be in-line or out of band and monitor the entire network. So proactively responds to events and can adjust traffic, it can do traffic shaping, it can shut down ports, it can log or alert if specific things happen, it can then turn on maybe different functions, it could start to capture traffic. It could perhaps turn on some type of decryption or inspection device to inspect SSL. So based upon certain things happening, it can proactively take action to make the network more secure, more functional, guard against errors, intrusions. Next, let's talk about something referred to as serverless architecture. With a serverless infrastructure, the underlying infrastructure is abstracted from the user. When you think of infrastructure-as-a-service or platform-as-a-service, IaaS or PaaS, those things abstract the infrastructure from the user. But now we're taking it even a step further and taking all of the infrastructure out of the picture, The only thing you have to worry about is the code. So only the code is managed and deployed, and that can scale at the individual call level. We no longer have to worry about spinning up instances of operating systems or infrastructure rack and stack, don't have to worry about the server at all. All we have to worry about is the function itself, and each individual function, each time it's called, that can scale independently. So having this in place allows you to only pay for the times that the function is called versus paying for an application to be always on and waiting for requests. IaaS and PaaS as an example, you pay for the infrastructure, you turn on a virtual machine, it's on, it's generating income for the host or for the hosting provider, because as long as that is on you're getting billed for it, whether it's used or not. If it spins up, obviously there's more cost associated, but simply having it turned on has a cost. When we do serverless architecture or when we do serverless computing, all we're worrying about is processing our functions, and we only pay for when that function actually gets called. Serverless providers, as an example, there's a few big ones out there. Amazon Web Services, AWS, has one called Lambda, Microsoft Azure has functions, and Twilio also has functions. There are three serverless providers for you to take a look at, maybe dig a bit deeper and understand more under the hood how these things work. It's beyond the scope to really dig too deep into it in this book, but just understand the basics of what serverless architecture is and how that can benefit you - the pros and cons versus things like IaaS or PaaS. To put all of these in context as to who manages what and where in the stack, we talked before about infrastructure-as-a-service. The first four layers, networking, storage, servers, and virtualization is managed by the vendor, and then you manage everything above that, operating system on up. Platform-as-a-service, it goes higher up the stack, then vendor manages most of that. You manage the functions, or the code, what's being called, in the application. When we're talking about function-as-a-service, or serverless computing, which is what we just talked about, the only thing that you're responsible for, or the only thing that you manage, is the function, the call itself. Everything else, the application, the runtime, middleware, all of the rest of the stack is managed by the vendor. Then we have software-as-a-service, or SaaS, and there everything is managed by the vendor. All you do is consume that service. So just understand all of the things that make up an application or make up a service, where they fit within this continuum, what parts you manage, and what parts the vendor manage.

Chapter 14 Service Integrations and Resource Policies

Next, a few more terms that I want you to be familiar with. We have services integration and resource policies. Services integration; many cloud providers provide services like database, network, maybe AI or ML, serverless or function-as-a-service, facial recognition, communication services, whether it's audio, video or messaging. Those services integration and all the other microservices associated with that, database connectivity, Amazon, Azure, the larger cloud providers, have thousands of microservices, and they're adding new ones all the time. Their services can be integrated with your applications. The only downside to keep in mind with these things is when you build an application in a specific cloud, like Amazon as an example, if you build it completely on their microservices architecture, for all the services that they provide, it becomes much more difficult to pull that application back out of that cloud. Not impossible, but it takes a lot of retooling. So just understand services integration where it fits in with the grand scheme of things. Does it lock you into that vendor? Does it make portability more difficult? Then when it comes to resource policies, so policies can be managed on-prem or in the cloud, and they can enable dynamic resource deployment, monitoring, management, asset reclamation. All of these policies can be defined, again locally, they can be just an on-prem thing, or if you have cloud integrations, you can integrate them with services, you can integrate them with policies, standardize where possible, make it as standard across the environment as possible, and that helps reduce risk and human error. Next, let's talk about a transit gateway. A transit gateway connects virtual private clouds, or VPCs, with on-premise networks. A transit gateway controls how traffic is routed among all the connected networks in what's known as a hub and spoke architecture. If we have a number of VPCs, virtual private clouds, we have a transit gateway connecting to a firewall, or a firewall/VPN, which then connects to a customer gateway and our customer network. It allows us to connect our network with

Amazon's cloud or Azure's cloud or Google's cloud, or put it in your cloud provider of choice, but it allows us to extend our network into that cloud network, and vice versa. Something else I want you to be familiar with is the concept of VM sprawl. VM sprawl is a large number of virtual machines on a network without proper IT management. This happens a lot of times because various departments and users will create their own virtual machines without proper procedures or lifecycle management. In other words, you may have a proof of concept, they may have a temporary project, or just trying things out, they'll spin virtual machines up, they forget that they're actually on and consuming resources. A few ways to avoid VM sprawl is define a virtual machine policy, so this boils down to strict IT policies around resource allocation and also their use. That will help ensure standardization and also awareness of assets. Next, create standard VM templates. Standardized templates help with providing users what they need, as well as proper naming conventions, and it makes it easier to identify VM owners, and also their purpose. Then implement lifecycle management, so ensure temporary or short-term resources are reclaimed on time to ensure that virtual machines aren't created and then forgotten about. We talked about spinning things up, and then they just sit there and consume resources. Then also, routinely audit, so auditing of the environment enables discovery of assets on the network and also works in tandem or facilitates proper lifecycle management. So don't just assume that we have these things in place, we have a policy in place, we have templates in place, all is well with the world. That's great, and that's obviously a great start, but we need to routinely audit to make sure those things are being adhered to, and then if things are spun up outside of those policies or outside of those templates, we capture that and then lifecycle them properly. A VM escape is an attack that enables the attacker to escape out of their VM, hence, the term VM escape, that allows them to bust out of jail. They're going to escape that VM and access resources on the actual host server. They could potentially interact with the host server or other VM guests being hosted on that server. If we have an attacker VM, VM2, VM3,

VM4. We have other guests on that host operating system. So, if that in fact happens, and the attacker in that VM is able to exploit a specific mapping function and is able to change where that mapping function points to back on the host OS, the host hardware, back on that server that it's actually running on, they can remap and jump from one VM to another. Resources on section 1 of that shared resource, they can remap from one to the other and then, in a sense, jump up into the other VM, and they can access resources in the other virtual machine, and also potentially access resources on the host itself. That's something to be concerned with. VMware, VirtualBox, Hyper-V, they're all aware of these things, and most of these vulnerabilities are mitigated as they come out. As we know, with any security threat, they're constantly evolving. You need to be aware of what VM escape is, what is currently available to mitigate these risks, and make sure that you're keeping an eye on your own environment to make sure these things are not introduced and running wild, or at least unchecked. Then you should check your own virtual infrastructure in your own virtual environment to make sure you're not susceptible to these types of attacks. In summary we talked about cloud models and their various types. We talked about managed service providers, and then fog and edge computing, the concept of each, and how they tie into cloud computing. We talked about microservices and APIs and how they function and make things interconnect, help us break large applications down into subcomponents and make them much more deployable and much more scalable. We also talked about Software-Defined Networking and Software-Defined Visibility, and then serverless architecture, and also virtualization.

Chapter 15 Environments, Provisioning & Deprovisioning

In the following chapters we'll be covering implementing secure application development, deployment, and automation. We'll be talking about the various types of environments. We're talking about testing, staging, QA and production. We'll be talking about provisioning and deprovisioning resources. We'll talk about integrity measurement and what that means. We'll talk about secure coding techniques and some things to keep in mind when coding for security. We'll talk about the OWASP specifications or the Open Web Application Security Project, along with software diversity, automation and scripting. We'll talk about elasticity, scalability, and also versioning control. Let's look at the various environments that we can deploy into. We have four we want to talk about here. We have development, we have testing, also staging, and then production. Depending upon the place you may work in, production may be all three of these for you. If at all possible, let's not have that situation. We want to have a separate environment we can test in, whether it's a virtualized environment. It could be small. It doesn't have to be an exact replication of production, but it should give us the ability to test separate from production so we don't affect things negatively. Let's talk about each of these in a little more detail. For development, that's we're going to do initiation and requirements gathering. So developers can work independently of each other in this environment. We're not necessary looking to have a big, gigantic team effort yet. We want our requirements gathered and then developers potentially working in independent work streams to that finished product. At some point, we'll collaborate and bring things together. But at the initial stages, they may be working in separate streams. The intent, is to eventually merge those streams into a combined system. Next, we have the test environment. Testing can take different forms and can be integrated throughout all phases. It's not necessarily a separate phase in and of itself. We should be testing along the way to make sure that we're meeting objectives. A testing environment is an area typically that's prior to or lower than a staging environment. Code usually runs on a single system or a very small or an isolated environment. Bugs are identified, processes and systems are modified, and resolved. This can be an iterative process that goes on and on again. The process doesn't have to be, but best results are achieved when that process is iterative. Next, we have staging. Staging is a production-like environment that we can use to test. We're going to test installation, configuration, and migration scripts. In staging, we may do performance testing. We may do load testing. We may have an application to do that. We may have a piece of infrastructure or a piece of hardware that would generate load, and we can turn it up or down, add additional users, add additional processes to make sure that our system that we're creating can actually handle that load, not just initially, but as things ramp up, as that system scales. Also any processes that are required by other teams, boundary partners, we want to test to make sure that we're not just developing in a vacuum. We want to make sure we're interoperating correctly with our boundary partners and with other teams to make sure the stuff that we do doesn't negatively impact them and vice versa. Then we have production. And production, as , is a fully functioning live environment. Most costly when errors are encountered here. This is the last place we want to encounter an error. We want to figure those things out in testing or staging if it all possible. Changes can be rolled out completely into production, or we can still do it in phases.

We can have pilot rollouts that still go into production, but it's going to a smaller group. It doesn't necessarily have to go across the board everywhere in one shot. It should go through change management. That change management board or that change management process should have a holistic view of all potentially competing changes taking place. Avoid change collisions aimed at the same system. You may work in a small environment. They may only have a few changes per night or a few changes per week. Or you could work in a very large enterprise that may have hundreds of changes or even thousands of changes per week. It just depends upon the environment, but the process is the same. There should be a group sitting on top of all of those changes to make sure that two different groups that may not even know about each other or the work that they're doing are going to impact a similar system. Additionally, they should know that the systems that are being modified, how they interrelate. That's where something like a CMDB or a configuration management database comes into play because if that is fully configured and fully populated, you can test or you can least look at the cascading impacts of changes That all the things, all the systems, applications, programs, infrastructure, how they all interrelate. If we go ahead and take a look at all these environments and we break them down or look at them and how they flow, we'll see that we have some Dev Teams here. This is going to be our development environment. We have Dev Team A, Dev Team B. And they may be working independently of each other at this point. They're not working at a cohesive system, they're working on individual components that will eventually be brought into and collaborate with to build some type of common system or some type of common end product. So from there you'll see there's a lot of interdependencies that are going on within those separate groups. They'll then take their work products and push those out to the QA Team. The QA Team then will go through its iterative testing process, and it will go through and look for functional dependencies and all the things that make the system at this point functional. It's either go or no go. It's very early in the process. They're looking at it, is it meeting the requirements at this point? From there, it gets pushed down to the test environment. The test environment does fully functional testing and system testing. You have a lot of client PCs, you'll see some laptops down here. They're going to be doing user testing, and they're testing against those databases, those systems, functionality overall. Those results get pushed up to a test results database where things are tracked. They will typically also get entered into some type of bug tracking system. That bug tracking system creates a feedback loop, and you can see it goes down and filters back into the development teams, and they can work through those bugs in an iterative process. Once it hits a certain stage, it then goes into staging. That's the final check area. That's where you'll look at all the piece parts and say, is the installation, the configuration, the scripts, any type of migration things, are all of those things fully functional? If they are, then it gets pushed into production for deployment. If not, it may go back to QA, it may go back to test. Depending upon what bugs are discovered, it may be an iterative process where it goes through this feedback loop over and over and over again, It may not be just a continuous stream from Dev to QA to test to staging the production, it may go from Dev to QA to test and back again and loop through for a number of cycles until it hits something that's then staging ready. Then from there it goes into production. Even at that point, when it goes into production, it may not go out to everybody at once. It may go on a pilot or a phased deployment. That way we're deploying to a small subset of our production users first, get their feedback, make sure everything is OK, we didn't miss anything, and then it gets rolled out to the larger production environment. Next, let's talk about provisioning and deprovisioning. What are we talking about here? Well, we're talking about commissioning and decommissioning. Bring something onto the floor or into our environment and then removing that thing from the environment. In this instance, we have a happy day - a new asset is installed. When we do that, we want to make sure we know when does that actual asset go end of life as well? We want to have an end-of-service date in mind, we want to do security scans, and we also need to have an MOP or a methods of operation for those daily operations or a runbook so we know how that asset functions and how it operates. Then also periodic auditing. We want to make sure all these things just set up. There's a cadence in place. There's processes in place to make sure that it's a methodical, predetermined process that we follow each and every time. Again, following things in a very systematic approach mitigates risk. It takes out the human error. Conversely, the sad day is when we're going to have that asset be decommissioned. We're not just going to push it off the dock and say farewell. We're going to go through a series of processes. All the data is migrated to a new platform, whether it's a server, whether it is a storage array, piece of infrastructure. Right now we're not talking about the DevOps model where we're treating servers or infrastructure more like actual livestock than pets. If something goes wrong, we don't worry about trying to figure things out. We don't log in and try to fix it. We just rip it out and put in a new one. We're talking about things here that are a little more substantial, potentially. That asset needs to be formally decommissioned. We'll determine does that data need to be migrated off to something new, or is that old data no longer needed? If so, the asset is wiped and purged as per policy. We want to use some type of wiping mechanism That data is not recoverable. Then the asset is disposed of properly. Now when we're talking about asset disposal, proper asset disposal is critical to maintain security and also to ensure that confidential data is removed. We have data wiping or purging, data wiping is different than just deleting. When we're wiping something, we're overwriting. Three, as per the Department of Defense or DOD, 5220.22-M, that is a guideline that says how many wipes or how many passes of a wiping mechanism actually secures that data beyond being recoverable. A three-pass wipe is an acceptable number of passes as per DoD standards. And then also an option would be the physical destruction of drives. We could throw them into a gigantic shredder and actually literally shred those drives.

Chapter 16 Integrity Measurement & Code Analysis

Next, let's talk about integrity measurement. It is an open source alternative that creates a measured runtime environment. We talked about TPM before. Well, this ties in with that. It creates a list of components that need to load. When we're booting our system, it's going to know exactly what needs to load and will not allow other things to load or be injected into that process. It's going to anchor that list to the TPM chip, we talked about that previously, to prevent tampering. That way it has a list. It's like when you walk into a club and the guy at the front door has a list, and if you're not on that list, you're not getting in. Well, very similar here. There's a list of things that can run. And if you're not on that list, it does not allow it. It blocks it from executing. That way it ensures that you have a secure environment upon bootup. What it also does is prevent sophisticated or targeted persistent attacks because, as we know, hackers can implement processes that will inject themselves very, very early in the boot process. It could potentially sit in the boot firmware or the master boot record of a device. As soon as that device boots up, that attack or that threat is already injected in the process, and they're already in before antivirus gets a chance to load, before other processes get to load. Ensuring that secure boot process prevents those injections from taking place, those persistent attacks from being actually injected into the system. We also have something referred to as the roots of trust. Now it's beyond the scope of this book really to dig into this, but I want you to be aware there's really three main components, a measurement, a storage, and reporting component. And what those things do, again, is tie into that root of trust or that boot process so that we know that everything that builds upon that is secure, or at least we can tell when that chain breaks down. If it starts off and the very beginning is compromised, then nothing after that can be guaranteed. So by having the roots of trust and having a measurement component, a storage component where those things are being stored securely, and reporting that we know if and when things change, it gives us the ability to start off securely and then go from there. Previously, we talked about static code analysis. That's also known as source code analysis. It's part of a code review process for something that's referred to as white-box testing. It allows you to see under the covers. It's also part of the implementation phase of the security development lifecycle or the SDL. It finds vulnerabilities in non-running code. It's static code analysis. We're looking for those vulnerabilities, either through taint analysis or data flow analysis. Data flow analysis is used to collect runtime or dynamic information about data in software while it's in a static state. Taint analysis, on the other hand, attempts to identify variables that have been tainted by user-controllable input and then traces that to possible vulnerable functions, also known as a sink. If a tainted variable gets past to a sink without first being sanitized, it gets flagged as a vulnerability. As I said, we're looking for vulnerabilities, looking for input, sanitization, looking for places where the user the ability to control that input. If they can put in something, this is where SQL injection and cross-site scripting attacks come into play, if they're able to use some type of technique, either as fuzzing or just straight up SQL injection, they can try every single possible combination of codes, letters, characters. If that is successful, that code does not get sanitized, it can crash a system or have unintended results. This data flow analysis and this taint analysis allows us to go in and really identify these things ahead of time. It's part of the defensive posture that we need to take as IT security professionals. Now does every IT security professional know all of these different things? No, not. There are areas of specialization obviously. But it's important for you to have a general concept and a general understanding, number 1, to know is this an area I want to go into. Number 2, even if it isn't, you need to have those conversations with the people that are responsible for this. And if you don't know about it, it's hard to have that conversation. As an IT security professional, it's important to have a good understanding of everything, not a deep dive, but a good understanding so who to talk to, who to coordinate with, whether they're developers, pen testers, coders, your DevOps folks, your IT security folks, your infrastructure folks, all the different lines of business . You can reach out to all these different areas, coordinate efforts, and make sure everyone is on the same page and everyone is working towards the same goal. Let's now talk about secure coding techniques. The goal of this chapter was not to make you a very highly-skilled coder. We're not deep diving into the actual nuts and bolts of coding here. But the general concepts, the general mindset behind the coding so that as an IT security professional, you can have those conversations with the DevOps folks and with the coders and make sure that these concepts are being followed. So secure coding techniques; proper error handling. We need to make sure the errors don't crash the system obviously, allow for elevated privileges, or expose unintended information. So having these discussions, again, with programmers and with coders, understand, ask the questions, show me how error handling works. Show me what happens if unintended input is entered. What happens if the system crashes? What does it actually give back to the end user? Proper input validation is another. We want to make sure that we sanitize the data to mitigate such things as cross-site scripting and cross-site forgery requests. If someone goes into a web portal, we want to make sure that data is sanitized they can't put in some rogue piece of information and get unintended results back. Also, normalization on the database back end. We want to ensure database integrity and optimization of data. Now you may ask yourself, what does this have to do with security? Well, normalizing the database ensures that there are no insertion or deletion anomalies. Downstream impacts might be if something gets deleted improperly or if something gets added improperly and now our database and our tables are out of sync, it could return unintended consequences or it could have unintended consequences and return unintended data. Normalization is key. Also we have stored procedures. We want to utilize vetted, secure procedures verses writing new code on the fly. Whenever possible, reuse code if appropriate or use stored procedures that have been vetted and are known to be secure. Next, code signing. We want to ensure that validated and trusted code is used. We want to mitigate risk from unsigned code being allowed to run because, again, if we allow things that have not been vetted, have not been signed, we don't know where that's coming from or we don't trust it. If we allow those things to run, we introduce risk, potential for malware, potential for spyware, ransomware, you name it, unintended results. Hackers can use these things to try to crash the system, inject code in the application. So unsigned code is a no no. Encrypting the data, that's going to mitigate the risk of compromise should the actual computer go missing, lost, or stolen, or the drives housing the data become lost or stolen. Then we have obfuscation or camouflage. This goes hand in hand with encryption. Masking the data, encryption is an example, to avoid detection by static code analysis. That typically involves such things as a decoder and the encoded payload. You can look at these things in one of two ways. Encryption is going to obviously keep the data out of prying eyes, but it also keeps someone from potentially reverse-engineering what we're doing. If we encrypting our code or obfuscating, otherwise camouflaging that code, they can't do static code analysis against that program and spot potential errors. It goes both ways. Those two things can either work for you or against you, depending upon which side of the fence you're sitting on. And then we have code reuse and dead code. Code reuse is simply code that can be reused, as the name implies, for some future use, future project. The challenge becomes when people try to write code that they can reuse later, they start to bring in things that may not be necessary for the project they're working on. They're trying to think of future uses or future bugs they might encounter or future issues they may come up with. They try to write code that is going to counteract those things when, in reality, they're probably not going to capture all those things anyway. But by focusing on what's right in front of you, you stand a much better chance of writing a very clean, secure piece of code. Server-side versus client-side. Take into account where validation, input sanitation, where those things occur and the way those controls can be bypassed. Server-side versus client-side depends upon where those things, where those validations and those sanitizations take place. They're easier to bypass on the client side than it is on the server side typically. Where we have the option, server side is typically better. Not always. There's always exceptions to every rule. But just some things to think about, so the conversations to have with the coders when you're discussing how the applications work and how they function. Next is memory management. That's going to ensure that code calls and manages memory properly to avoid heap and buffer overrun errors. These things could cause the system to crash. They could cause system instability, data exposure. things to ask your developers, making sure you're both on the same page, making sure they've thought through these things, which they may or may not have. It's always good do actually validate. Don't just assume that because someone works on code that they knew how to do it securely. There's obvious conversations that need to be had. Then third party libraries and SDKs or software development kits. Ensure that you understand any third party, any third party's security requirements, their vetting processes, where their data is stored, interaction with other apps, data. Don't just assume that they have the same level of security that you do. Always vet that, and remember that security is only as strong as the weakest link. Make sure that there is some type of service level agreement or an understanding between companies how they vet their process, how they take security as a consideration. Is their security up to the level of yours because it doesn't matter how strong your security is if there's this week, if an attacker is able to come in through the side door through their weaker security and then pivot and come through into your application or your network, that poses a challenge, and, a breach can occur. Then lastly, we have data exposure. What types of data are exposed? If unexpected inputs are put into the system and it causes a system to crash or causes some unintended result or what errors are returned if incorrect data is entered. In other words, if someone puts in some type of string or they try cross-site scripting or cross-site forgery request or they go through some type of fuzzing exercise where they just try every single combination of characters and letters to see what happens to see if the system crashes, if and when it does crash, what types of information are returned? Does it tell you the operating system, the kernel version, all those things an attacker could potentially use to fingerprint this system. Or if the website, as an example, asked for a username and password, and they put in the wrong username, does it tell them, hey, this username is not valid. Well, that lets them know, hey, strike that from the list. That one's not valid. Let's try the next one. It allows them to brute force that versus if it simply says, hey, this was correct, you'll get an email back or an email was sent or some type of more ambiguous error message so it doesn't give them any insight into what's valid or not valid. It's all a matter of conversations that you should have with the coders and developers to make sure that everyone is on the same page. They will then understand how security factors in, and you will get a better understanding of how the applications interact with each other.

Chapter 17 Security Automation, Monitoring & Validation

Security automation it's automating the processes of implementing rules, enforcing policies, and making changes. It's based on triggers and policy violations. If things happen, or when things happen, other things will get triggered and fired off and come into play automatically. It doesn't require a security administrator to be sitting there watching a monitoring station or some type of management station to see, hey, this happened, let me shut down that port, let me turn on this service, let me audit this, or look at that. Everything is done in an automated fashion. It's repeatable, it's deterministic, and it allows for things to scale pretty quickly. It can also reduce time to remediate, again, because everything is done automatically. It can mitigate risk, because things are now repeatable. It's going to mitigate that risk of human error. The other thing to keep in mind, however, though, for every plus there's also a con, for every good thing, there's a potential exploit, It can also be exploited and shut things down Denial-of-Service attacks, if the attacker knows what they're doing, and they say, I know for a fact if I do this, these four or five things are going to happen. Well, if I flood that specific thing, it's going to cause the system, because it's operating in an automated fashion, it could cause that system to overload, to shut down ports, to really take a service down when there really wasn't a need to do that. There's a constant refinement of that process to make sure we're not over-engineering, and we're not shutting things down unnecessarily or taking measures that aren't necessarily appropriate. However, for the most part, this is a very good way to approach security because, again, it allows you to scale and reduces that human error. As an example, let's say, for instance, we have a firewall change. That firewall change is reviewed and approved by some human, so they're going to look at it and say, go for it. That change gets logged. Now here's where the automation kicks in. Instead of someone having to do all these things manually, this process can be done in an automated fashion. As soon as that change is logged, it can initiate a security scan. That scan could then go out and initiate or turn on some remote instance, some remote network scan instance, which is going to do a remote network scan, . That's going to all be done automated. It's going to then take the output of that scan, compare with a known good, and make sure that the changes were, in fact, proper, and didn't have any downstream impact, downstream effects. Then, if everything looks good, those changes are logged in the ticketing system. Instead of having to go through a process where everyone has to sign off on that workflow piece by piece, this can all be done in an automated fashion, and this can all be done in minutes instead of potentially hours or even days. Next, we need to make sure that we have continuous monitoring. Continuous monitoring is going to increase visibility. It allows us to see end-to-end what's happening within that workflow. Because when we're doing things in an automated fashion, we don't necessarily have the ability for personnel to be stopping every so often and actually catch some type of error in the process. Continuous monitoring allows us to ramp up scale and volume while still making sure we're catching any errors, quality assurance. It also reduces errors and false positives. If we're monitoring everything along the process, and we know it's a very deterministic workflow, it's going to give us the same output each and every time, any deviation from that allows us to catch it very, very quickly. It also reduces our time to resolution, because if we catch something the moment it happens, we can fix it very, very quickly. It doesn't sit there and fester or turn into something larger, have greater downstream impacts. Something that goes hand-in-hand with that is configuration validation. Configuration validation and management is key to success at scale. There are things that we need to make sure are in place to allow us to catch any configuration drift, any things that start to go off course. Things like Puppet, Chef, Ansible, and Salt are a few of the tools that are typically used in this type of environment as orchestration and automation tools to allow us to make sure we have configurations in place, and any configuration drift gets put back to its known good state very quickly. Next, we have continuous integration. This is merging developer updates continuously, daily in this case, to avoid integration challenges because if we take a piece of code and we have developers work on that in a vacuum and they spend days or perhaps even weeks working on a piece of code, and you have three or four developers working in silos, and then you try to integrate those changes back into some mainstream code base, if everyone is doing so many different changes, trying to integrate that in, it's going to be extremely problematic if not impossible. Having this very continuous stream, this iterative back and forth, code updates are done very quickly. They're integrated back into the main codebase very quickly. It allows things to move forward in a very automated or semi-automated fashion. Waiting too long integrate can cause codebase to get out of sync. That's typically a result of multiple developers working at the same time. Integrate early and integrate often. That is the key to success in this model. Automated testing processes and also a replica of production or as close as you can to production is really critical to success. What I mean by testing automation is every time a change, when you have these developers working on various pieces of code, as soon as those code changes are committed to the main codebase, that should trigger a new test that should automatically be built. A new testing process kicks off, and that automated fashion allows you to quickly iterate, quickly get a new test in place, make sure that everything is validated. That is the new normal or the new committed codebase. We can go back through the process again, introduce any other changes or tweaks and modifications, and again test it over and over again. You see the infinite loop sign. That's really what it is. It's a continuous back and forth, making sure that changes get integrated quickly and moved forward. Next we have continuous delivery. Continuous delivery is an extension of continuous integration. What it is as an automation of the actual release process, in addition to the automated testing, the continuous integration. We're taking that one step further and automating the actual release of those changes or those tweaks. These actual deciding on the release frequency, however, is a manual process, We still decide when to actually do the release. We still push the button, if you will. Whether that's hourly, daily, weekly, that schedule is determined manually. On the other hand, if we look at continuous deployment, well, that takes continuous delivery one step further and automates the entire process. All changes that pass all stages of the pipeline are automatically released to the customer. The feedback loop is accelerated, and also it allows developers to focus on building software. As they push changes, as it makes its way through the CI/CD pipeline and it passes through the different testing phases, QA, staging, tests, as soon as it passes all those things, it's automatically released to the customer. If we look at this continuous delivery versus continuous deployment, we have our continuous integration area, we have builds and test, and we're going to look at a comparison between the two. In a continuous delivery model, we have our builds and test, and it passes through the various stages, acceptance, deploy to staging. Deploy to production you'll notice is different because that's going to be a manual process. When we decide, hey, we're ready to push this change, we hit the button, deploy it to production, and then we initiate our smoke tests. On the other hand, in continuous deployment, the acceptance test, deploy to staging. Deploy to production you'll notice is the same because one was a manual process, but now we do it automatically. As soon as the change is initiated, it makes its way through the different stages in our pipeline and is automatically released to production. That way, those changes get pushed almost in real time, and feedback can also be delivered in almost real time to allow very quick and also very iterative changes to be pushed to the environment and allow modifications, enhancements to be delivered much more quickly. Now let's talk about an organization that I want you to be familiar with, and that is OWASP. And that is the Open Web Application Security Project. It's an open community that produces articles, methodologies, documentation, tools, and other various technologies in the field of web application security. I don't want to dig too deep into them at this point, but I want you to be aware of who they are and then also provide you with a link that you can dig in and learn a little more about the organization. And also, here's a link to a quick reference guide they produce to give you a quick checklist of things that revolve around web application security. https://owasp.org

Chapter 18 Software Diversity, Elasticity & Scalability

Next we have software diversity. This boils down to creating different variations internally to a program to make it harder to reverse-engineer or harder to attack because the internal workings are different each and every time the application runs or at least for different users. We're creating functionally equivalent, but internally different variants of a program. Users get diversified variants of a particular program, and it makes understanding the inner workings of the application more difficult, which in turn makes attacking that application much more difficult. There's two parts to that. One is the compiler, and the compiler takes high-level source code, and it transforms it into low-level machine code. And when it does that, it diversifies that machine code, making the attack more difficult. Each time it runs, it changes it slightly, making it more difficult to actually interact with. The attackers don't know exactly how things work. The other side of that is the binary or the binaries. Introducing randomness into the binaries, either through NOPs, or no operations, and also scheduling randomization. By doing this, we're actually not changing the way it actually works, just the timing, just the way the things operate under the hood. But all of the valid constructions, all of the valid things are still there. We're just injecting some randomness. Maybe it's timing, maybe it's scheduling, maybe it's even memory addresses. But by doing so, the attacker has no clear line of sight as to craft a specific attack for that specific operation or that specific program because every time it runs or at least for every user, it's going to be slightly different. Next, we have elasticity and scalability. This is the ability to grow or reduce on demand and reduces risk because it does a few things. It takes away stranded capital because we don't necessarily have to buy a bunch of stuff that we don't necessarily need. We don't have to buy for our maximum in other words. We know we're going to get 20,000 users once a year, but we don't have to buy equipment to scale to 20,000 users when we only have to do that maybe one week out of the year. The rest of the year, we may only have 2,000 users. It eliminates the need for stranded capital and investing more than is necessary. Then, conversely, we don't have to worry about not having enough to scale when necessary. We buy to our minimums and then don't have enough to scale when the maximums hit. It achieves really both purposes. Also, we can instantiate additional security or cloud monitoring, distributed denial-of-service protection as needed. We don't necessarily have to have a lot of these protections in place, overload if you will, all year round. We may want to do it around specific events. Or when certain things are triggered, we can then fire up additional resources to protect us or to monitor or do whatever for that period of time and then scale back when not necessary. That way we're not paying for things that we don't need. To wrap things up, let's talk about versioning control. Version control allows developers to work on projects together. A version control system will track all changes to code. As multiple developers are working on something, every change will get tracked and stored as a separate version. It maintains the history of all changes, it allows for a rollback, and it allows you to make a mistake and roll back to a prior version or also fork a specific line of code and maybe go in a divergent path. Where those forks occur, you could roll back prior to that change. Version control repositories or repos can be centralized or distributed, and GitHub is perhaps the most common version control system. If we look at centralized versus decentralized, there's two major differences. In a centralized system, we have users who will actually push all of their code, all of their changes, up to a centralized server. They must maintain network connectivity. They have to be attached to the server. Every time they want to make a change or receive a change, it goes up to the server, and then the users access the change from that centralized server. Everything is stored in a central repository. Conversely, in a decentralized environment, we have users connecting to a server. But there's a copy of the project, and all the changes and all the history of that project is actually pushed out to each individual user. They have a copy on their desktop or their laptop, It gives you additional copies, redundancy. It's also much faster because you're not relying on network speed, network connectivity. It also allows people to work offline. Two different approaches achieving the same thing. Decentralized is perhaps the more popular version. Most open source projects will be using a decentralized repository as well. Just keep that in mind. In your shop, your company, your development area, you definitely should be using some type of version control to make sure that changes are tracked, and you can also roll back when issues are discovered. In summary we talked about environments, the various environments like testing, staging, QA, production. We talked about provisioning and deprovisioning of assets on projects. We talked about integrity measurement. We talked about secure coding techniques, the Open Web Application Security Project or OWASP. We talked about software diversity, automation and scripting, and then elasticity, scalability, and then, lastly, version control.

Chapter 19 Directory Services, Federation & Attestation

In the following chapters we'll be talking about Authentication and Authorization Methods. We'll be talking about authentication methods and the various technologies associated with that. We'll talk about smartcard authentication, biometrics, also talk about multi-factor authentication, or MFA. We'll talk about authentication, authorization, and accounting, otherwise known as AAA, and then also cloud versus on-premise requirements, as far as authorization and authentication is concerned. First up is directory services. Directory services provides authorization and also authentication for computers, for users, and also for groups, so laptops, desktops and servers. A component of that is something referred to as LDAP or lightweight directory access protocol. LDAP is the language or the protocol that is actually used to talk to Active Directory. They're not one and the same. Active Directory is the authentication mechanism or the suite of tools behind the scenes that Microsoft uses for their domains and networks. LDAP is a protocol that could be used to talk to Active Directory. LDAP could also talk to other authentication services as well. So real quick, without digging too deeply into Active Directory here, we'll talk about LDAP, we'll talk about Kerberos in other chapters, but just to brief history on Active Directory. Active Directory was developed in 1999 and introduced in 2000, and it was introduced with, as you guessed it, Windows 2000. In 2003, it was built upon, and we added the ability to change the position of domains within forests, within AD forests or Active Directory forests. Fast-forward to 2008, we added Active Directory Federated Services, or ADFS. And Active Directory itself was rebranded to Active Directory Directory Services and added some additional security features like PAM or privileged access management. Then in 2016, again, fast-forwarding through some of these iterations, Windows Server 2016 released Azure AD to enable the joining of on-prem Active Directory or on-prem AD with Azure AD. This enabled SSO or single sign-on for MS cloud services like Office 365 . Active Directory or AD has been evolving since it was first introduced in 2000. As far as a username is concerned, just so we're clear, every operating system creates user names for each user of a system. Each username is assigned a unique ID. For instance, in Windows in Active Directory, that unique ID is called a SID, or a security identifier. That is actually how the computer identifies that user, not the username. Without digging too deeply into the nuts and bolts of Active Directory, the username is the human-readable form. Well, if I create that user, he gets assigned a SID. If I delete that user and then recreate him again, same usernamer, he'll be given actually a different SID, or a different security identifier. It's better to disable an account and then later on re-enable that account, if you need to give it access again. Next we have federation, and a federation is allowing access to company resources to outside parties. so we're going to federate with other groups. A trusted third party is going to be that authentication mechanism, and they're going to authenticate the client, or the host, or the user, or whatever your terminology is, so that if two people trust this trusted third party, if I trust so and so, and the person I want to give access to also trust so and so, this third party, then we can both agree that we're going to allow that communication to occur because we both trust the person that we've both authenticated to. Social media sites like Facebook, Twitter, they all provide federation services. You may have logged in at some point in time to a website, that's not really Facebook or Google, but you actually log in with your Facebook, or Google, or LinkedIn password, your Twitter password, that provides that federated service. It allows you to authenticate and then log into that other web service because you both trust whatever it is, Facebook or Twitter. A trust is something that exists between two parties, two domains to companies. Well, we have such things as a one-way trust. Well that is company A trusts company B, but company B does not trust company A. It's a one-way street. It's a one-way street that they live on. Two-way street or two-way trust rather is A trusts B and also B will trust A. Company A is going to trust company B. And in return, company B is going to trust company A. Then we have a non-transitive trust where company A trusts company B, but it does not allow that trust to extend beyond company B. Company B, in other words, could not allow companies C or D to also trust A. It's a non-transitive trust. It does not go beyond the barriers and the parameters that were initially set. Then we have a pure transitive trust where A trusts B, B is going to trust C, and so A trusts C by virtue of transitivity. If we look at this graphically, we have host A. We have host B and host C. Well host A is going to trust host B. Host B is going to trust host C. So by virtue of transitivity, host A will also trust host C. It passes through transitively through host B. Our next concept of attestation. Attestation is used to prove that a system is secure and operates from a secure code base. This includes support for a Hardware Root of Trust, and what it does is it enables a service to securely sign the attestation data to prove that the device is the originator of the request. The TPM chip, the hardware chapter we talked about previously, or a trusted execution environment, they're examples of chips, or a secure area, so let's say, for instance, a secure enclave on an iPhone, as an example, it's an area that really can't be tampered with, and what it does is establishes that Hardware Root of Trust. Everything that flows down from that can be assumed to be secure.

Chapter 20 Time-Based Passwords, Authentication & Tokens

Next, we have something referred to as TOTP or a time-based, one-time password. TOTP is a unique password that uses a time-based algorithm to generate that password. As an example, we have a client trying to log into a server, and they're going to use something called Google Authenticator in this example, but there are a number of different tools that can provide the same type of functionality. But if you look at this a little more closely, we'll see here that we have the user wants to log into a server. They're going to log in with their username and their password. That server will then turn around and challenge them with that time-based, one-time password. As an example, an app for your phone, Google Authenticator, RSA makes one. There are a number of different companies and utilities that are available, but they'll all use similar algorithms. It will create a one-time password that lasts for either 30 seconds or 60 seconds, again, depending upon the utility. That will be unique for that short period of time. It's time based. But that also is in sync with the authentication mechanism on the server. Those two numbers as they regenerate and they change every 30 seconds or every 60 seconds, it's going to change both on that application and also on the server. So once the user enters his username and password correctly and gets challenged with the TOTP, the time-based, one-time password, he's going to put in his own pin into that authenticator, which allows him to then access. It's going to pop up and give him that six-digit pin or that six-digit number. He'll in turn enter that in. Then if it matches on the server, assuming that it does, the service or the server rather will grant access to that resource. Next we have HOTP, and it's a hash message authentication code algorith, HMAC for short. HMAC-based one-time password. That's the open standard for OAuth, similar to what we just talked about previously with the TOTP, or a time-based one-time password, and we can use the Google Authenticator as the same type of tool in that example. You can have different HMAC-based one-time passwords for different services, whether you're logging into email, or a server, or Dropbox, or whatever it is that online service is, or maybe a VPN for work, that will change every X number of seconds and can be used to maintain separate accounts, separate HMACs for each individual account, and as you go in and put your password in, it will regenerate every 60 seconds, you get the one that you need and are on to that server, and it will give you access, to that service. Also something to keep in mind is the fact that SMS can be used as a two-factor authentication mechanism as well. A user registers a mobile device with a service or a website, or whatever it is you're trying to access, and then when logging in, the user will provide that username and password. But then the service, the website, or the application will send a one-time code. You'll typically verify your mobile number, either like the last four digits, or click on a drop-down button or radio button that verifies your phone number. That SMS push then takes place, and a one-time code is sent as an added layer of security. That way, it's something that , and it's also something that you have, the phone in your possession. Now you have a one-time code you can use to log into that website. A similar functionality can also be provided via an automated phone call. Sometimes you have the option of choosing an SMS text message, or you can have that same service call your phone and leave you a voice message with that one-time code. Another authentication mechanism is something referred to as a token. A token is an authentication mechanism that can identify and also authenticate. I can tell servers or resources what access rights a user possesses. It can also allow or deny access. In a simplified example, but let's say, for instance, we have a user who wants to access a resource, in this case they want to access a server on their network. Well, they've already logged into the network, they've authenticated with Active Directory. Active Directory then gives them a token, and that token says what you can and cannot access, what groups you belong to. When they go to access that resource, they pass along that token. That token, in effect, has a number of different attributes. the user SID, the group SIDs, any security IDs of groups they're actually a member of, privileges, what's their primary group, the default ACLs, or access control lists, a number of attributes that's presented to the server, the server will look at that and say Active Directory says you have access, so you may pass, and then access, is granted, or if they're not a member of the group or there's an explicit deny, then access would be denied. Another method of authentication is static codes. Static codes are backup codes, essentially, that can be created and stored as a backup, or for a one-time use. Depending upon the application or the service, you may be given a number of backup code that you can print, take offline, store somewhere safe, That way if you lose your phone or your authentication device, your authentication mechanism, Google Authenticator, or whatever it is that you had initially set up, if that's gone, you can use these backup codes to actually get back into your account. Many password managers and also security applications will enable a user to generate a list of offline or backup codes, and then again, you print them and store them offline. That way, they're there in case of an emergency. Next is the actual authentication application, which we talked about before.

But these authentication applications can create a one-time password, an HMAC password, Applications that generate a code every X number of seconds or minutes, perhaps 30 seconds or every 60 seconds, so they're in sync with the application being logged into or the web server being logged into. Your application is in sync with the one on the web server or the application you're logging into, and it will change every X number of seconds. An RSA Token or a key fob was an early example of this; however, nowadays, many Android and also IOS apps have this functionality as well. Authy is one for iOS, Google Authenticator, Microsoft Authenticator. There a number of them out there. They all work very similarly, and they can generate these passwords independent of each other. Each account will have their own synchronization and their own actual backup codes. Some might be six digits, some might be 8, some might be 10. Something similar would be a push notification. A push notification is authentication that validates a login attempt by sending an access request to an associated mobile device. When I register my account, I will link it to a mobile device that I own. Instead of entering a password, I receive an access request notification within the application itself, which I then can approve or deny. As an example, if I try to log into Gmail via a web browser, it will actually push an access request to my Gmail application on my phone, and it pops up a notification and says, hey, someone's trying to log into your account, is this you, yes or no, do you authorize it? I can either say, no, it's not me. If someone else is trying to do it, it gives me an alert. Or I could say yes, and all I have to do is push the yes button and then I log into the website. It saves me from having to put in a pin or any of that type of stuff. I just log in with my username or email address and password, and then I get a push notification to finish the process.

Chapter 21 Proximity Cards, Biometric & Facial Recognition

Let's now cover physical access control. Smart cards give us access control, and it's also a security device. It contains a small chip or an amount of memory on that card, and that card can contain information about us. It could be metadata about who we are, it could contain medical records, it could contain access, as far as like what doors we can access within a building. Also, different levels of authorization or authentication for network resources. User permissions, access information. It's alTypically combined with multi-factor authentication, such as a PIN or a password. One is something that you have, the other is something that . For it to be true two-factor authentication, it has to be from separate categories. We can set it up so that incorrectly entering a PIN or password "X" number of times can even shut that card down and render it invalid. That way, if it's stolen and someone's trying to just randomly brute force their way in, that will shut things down and not allow that to happen. Two types of proximity cards are RFID and also NFC. RFID is the earlier version, although still very much widely in use, and then NFC is the newer version. The RFID cards that most people are familiar with allow for such things as security access into a building, even passing through a toll booth. NFC, or Near-Field-Communication, is more or less the evolution of RFID. That has roughly about a 4-inch range, It makes it a little bit more secure. You have to be actually very close to the proximity device you want to scan or connect to, make a payment through. Apple Pay, Google Wallet, Samsung Pay, all these things that uses NFC type of chip or NFC type of communication allow for very close proximity, so you have to be roughly 3 to 4 inches away from the reader. You put your phone up to it, and then it prompts you to either enter a fingerprint, or a password, or something that you may have that will then make that purchase or send that payment. If someone is standing 5 feet away or 10 feet away, they're not going to be able to intercept that because the range on these things are only roughly about 4 inches. They can also be used to transfer any type of data. With the Apple platform, or iOS, it's really only used for payments, but it could also be used for transferring video files, contact information, so NFC has a lot of uses beyond just making mobile payments. Next we have a personal identification verification card, or a PIV, and that's actually issued by the United States Federal Government. It's a smart card. It has a chip, and that chip contains encrypted information about that person. It also has a barcode, and it can display various pieces of information, their photo, what branch of the service they work for, or what specific department they're involved with. There may also be things like pay grade or their rank and issue date and an expiration date. And all of these things are actually contained also in the bar code and also in that smart chip. This will grant that cardholder access to federal facilities and information systems. It's established by the Federal Information Processing Standard 201, or FIPS. These cards are used extensively throughout federal facilities throughout the U.S. Next, we have a common access card, and this is similar to the PIV we talked about previously. It's a smart card issued by the Department of Defense, and it's a general identification mechanism used for accessing DoD computers, signing email. We have a picture of the card on the front and the back. It has the barcode and a smart chip, the integrated chip that you see there. This particular card lists paygrade, rank, affiliation, expiration date, and the federal ID. On the back, it has very similar information. It has some additional pieces of information such as blood type, DoD benefits number, date of birth and so on. These cards are capable of containing quite a bit of information about a specific individual. Definitely something that can be used for authentication. Next, let's talk about biometric factors. A fingerprint scanner allows someone to uniquely identify themselves with their fingerprint, and as we know, fingerprints are, for the most part, considered unique, although, again, depending upon where you read. But for all intents and purposes, they are unique right. It measures multiple points and multiple factors on the fingerprint and uniquely identifies that person. Then we have retinal scanners and iris scanners where it actually goes in and reads the back of the eye, or the inside of the back of the eyeball, the retina, or an iris scanner looks at the pattern within the iris itself, and that will be unique to that person. We also have voice recognition where it can ask you to repeat a certain phrase or a passphrase over and over again, and it will learn your voice, and you can use that voice as your password. All of these things are great conveniences, although some of those can potentially be bypassed rather quickly. For instance, on an iOS device, your fingerprint scanner, well, if you're sleeping and someone walks up and grabs your thumb and puts it on your phone, they can unlock it pretty quickly, so not necessarily foolproof; however, that fingerprint is unique to you. It doesn't necessarily mean it can't be used to unlock your phone even without your knowledge. When it comes to biometrics, one of the first things that people think about is fingerprints. But there's also facial recognition, and that's comprised of software that can detect a person's identity based upon facial characteristics. New or 3D technologies have increased the accuracy, and also use cases range from government, commercial, and also consumer applications. There's use cases where we scan crowds at sporting events, concerts, also government buildings, and then also, once we've had actual incidents, terrorist activities facial recognition has been used to scan a crowd and try to pull people out of those large crowds and those large gatherings. Some potential weaknesses with facial recognition are low resolution photos, it's very hard to get things when it's grainy or pixelated, also changes in appearance. Whether it's a beard, a hat, scarves, sunglasses, all of those things can also inhibit facial recognition accuracy. Also, drastic changes in facial expressions can have an effect as well. Then we have anti-facial recognition technology, so reflective glasses, infrared emitting glasses, it gets a little bit crazy. But, whatever technology comes out, there's obviously a group or an industry that pops up as well to try to thwart those activities or try to thwart that technology. There's always a battle. But just understand that the technology is there currently, it's getting better and better all the time, but it's not foolproof, and we'll talk about error rates in just a moment.

Chapter 22 Vein and Gait Analysis & Efficacy Rates

The next one I want to bring your attention is vein analysis. It's a biometric authentication using the vein or the vein pattern in a human finger, so a user would insert a finger into what's called an attester terminal, like a fingerprint reader, That emits near-infrared LED. The hemoglobin in blood absorbs that near-infrared LED light, and the patterns are unique to each individual, and they're almost impossible to counterfeit because they are underneath the skin. As you can imagine, very, very difficult and potentially very painful to try to counterfeit. Next, we have something we refer to as gait analysis. This is identifying a person based upon their unique walking pattern. I can imagine in your head right now, you're saying, man, this is getting crazy. We're identifying people by every single characteristic you can possibly imagine, and the reality is, unfortunately, yes, we're becoming more and more surveilled. It has good implications and also bad implications, but something that you need to be aware of is there are new technologies and new capabilities constantly being developed. That can be things like step length, walking speed, it could be cycle time parameters like joint rotation of the hip, the knee, and the ankle, the angles of the thigh, the foot, the trunk. All of these things combined are unique to an individual. It can help to identify that person, whether just by walking singularly, or in a crowd. Potential use cases would be, before with facial recognition, would be criminal justice applications or national security applications. Three things you should be aware of. We have something referred to as a FAR, or false acceptance rate, and this is the probability that the system will incorrectly authorize a non-authorized person. It's giving someone access that shouldn't have it. Next, we have a false rejection rate, or FRR. That's the probability that the system incorrectly rejects an authorized person. That's not quite as much of an issue as a false acceptance rate, both are not good, but it's better to reject someone that should be there than to allow someone in that shouldn't, but neither are ultimately acceptable. Then next we have a crossover error rate, or CER. That's the rate where both accept and reject error rates are equal. If we have the crossover error rate, we have the error rate on one axis, and then we have the sensitivity of that application with the technology on the other axis. We have the false acceptance rate, and then we also have the false rejection rate. Well, the point where those things meet, where they're both equal, a properly-tuned system should have equal false rejection rates and also false acceptance rates. If one is higher than the other, then the system is not tuned properly, and we need to make sure that that application is functioning properly. Let's now define what the differentiation is between identification, authentication, and authorization. Sometimes they're used interchangeably, but there really are three discrete things. But, what's the difference? Identification is who you are. Sounds like a no brainer, but in a nutshell, that's what it is. That means labeling a person via a username, a security ID, via smart card, PIV, so on, but who that person is, what we label that person as. Next is authentication, and that is actually proving who you are, and that can be a username and password combo, a pin, an OTP or a one-time password, biometric data. you say I'm so and so, or I say I'm so and so, anybody could call themselves anything, but how do you prove that, and that's by authenticating. And then we have authorizations, and that deals with permissions. So once you've said who you are and we've authenticated, we've proved who we are, now what can I do? So once I prove that I am administrator, what rights and permissions do I have on that system or on that network? That's really what that points to, what you're allowed to access once your authenticated, authorization happens after authentication. Next is authentication and just at a high level, just give you a quick overview, authentication is going to be the process of validating an identity. That is proving that you are who you say you are. If you say you're user A, or user B, or user C, prove it. Let's validate that. That could be something like a fingerprint, it could be a password, or a PIN. It's something that , or have, or whatever that's unique to you that's going to validate that you are who you say you are. The concept of multifactor authentication is something you should be familiar with. Multifactor authentication is two or more pieces of information that is used to authenticate someone. It could be a PIN. It could be a password, a fingerprint or a retina scan. But here's the caveat, it must be from different categories. A password and a PIN would really only be considered one factor of authentication because both fall under something . Things like what you have, what , what you do, where you are, but it has to be from two or more categories for it to be true multifactor authentication. Next, we have authentication factors, and these are the things you have to have in place for a multi-factor authentication system to function, something that , which could be a password or some secret, then there's something that you have, and that could be a smart card, or a token, or some type of dongle, maybe a USB dongle that changes every X number of seconds, or it could be something that you are, and that refers to a fingerprint, a retina scan, some type of biometric data. To have a true multi-factor authentication system, we have to make sure that we have at least two things that are in separate categories. We may have something that , in other words, some type of shared secret or password, along with a smartcard or a token. Having a password and a pin, if we had both of those together, that's only a single factor, because they're both something that we know. We know the password. We know the pin, but yet, if we have a password and something that changes every 60 seconds, that's something that we have. If we know, a password plus that, then we have two-factor authentication. Or if we had that same password and perhaps our fingerprint or a retina scan, that again would be multi factor because we have something from something that and also from something that you are. Two other authentication factors that I want you to be aware of is, number one, somewhere you are, so that's location based, in other words. An IP address, geolocation, it could be a specific place on the map, or it could be a specific place in a building, a floor, so forth or an IP address, so you can only log in or a session is locked to a specific IP address. Then also, we have something you do, and that could be a signature, a handwriting analysis, as an example, a pattern of behavior, the way you type, certain misspellings, language or slang. This is more of an emerging field, and depending upon who you talk to, could be considered more art than science, but it has been proven to be very accurate. People typically will do the same types of things over and over again, same types of spelling mistakes, the speed at which they type, the certain words that they use, the slang. All of these things could be used to, not only identify you, but to also authenticate you. Next is authorization, and authorization defines what you're allowed to access. That happens after you're authenticated. Remember, we prove, we identify, then we authenticate, and then we authorize. That authorization occurs after you're authenticated, and it can be controlled via policy, whether it be Group Policy in the Windows environment or some other type of policy mechanism in other operating systems, and it just says who can access what. It could be such things as time of day restrictions. It could be length of time restrictions, so we could only allow someone to log into our network between, let's say, 6 A.M. and 5 P.M. That way, if they happen to come in or try to come in at midnight, as an example, they would not be allowed. Or we could say, once they're on our system, they're only allowed to be on there for an 8-hour period. If they're on there longer than that, then they get booted. Then we also have file and folder access rights. What files can I access? What folders can I access? What resources, what printers, and so on. Two other authentication factors that I want you to be familiar with, and these are relatively new and not necessarily widely accepted across the board, but two of these you should be familiar with, nonetheless. That is, something that you exhibit. And that could be a personality trait, a neurological trait. We've talked about things getting crazier and crazier when we're trying to identify people. Well, this just goes along that same path. Obscure use cases at this point, but it is something that you should be aware of, personality traits, neurological traits, something that you may exhibit that is unique to you. Then also, someone that . That could be social proof. Having a friend or a colleague vouch for a user, usually via some type of token generation. When you create your account, you may designate someone as a friend or someone that can vouch for you in the event that you lose your credentials. You can then reach out to that person, or they will be sent some type of notification that says, hey, the person that you vouched for has lost their credentials; please provide authorization to allow them into their account. You can set that up ahead of time, That way, they're a, in case of an emergency break glass type of person, that they can allow you back into your account. Lets round this section up with authentication, authorization, and accounting, otherwise known as AAA. Authentication, as we've talked about before, identifies the user and allows or denies access or challenges for additional credentials, such as a pin, or a rotating code, a one-time password that will allow you to authenticate. From there, you have authorization, so that provides things like the length of time allowed on a network, access-control lists, or ACLs, for various resource is, what you're actually allowed to access. And then we have accounting, so that tracks the start and stop time of each session, and that can be used for billing or showback. Accounting is used by ISPs, service providers to track how long you've been online and how much they can bill you for. Next, we have on-prem versus cloud requirements when we're talking about authorization. For on-prem, it's locally managed authentication - something you have direct control over. All users and resources are housed under "one roof", and it could be a geographically dispersed or a multi-building facility, but it's still under one roof as far as under that company's auspices. Then we have onboarding and off-boarding must be properly maintained and optimized to avoid shadow IT. We don't want little small groups sprouting up all over the place and authorizing their own users, giving access to resources. That should be done collectively under one management organization. And then we have IT admins must also maintain all networking, configuration, lifecycle, integration. That can be problematic, and it's also a recurring thing every few years - two, three years, five years, depending upon your lifecycle, you have to go through that exercise all over again. Then if you have your infrastructure staggered It's not all up for refresh at the same time, then it's going to be a yearly process over and over and over again. One benefit though being it's potentially more flexible and more customizable, which, depending upon how you look at it, could be a blessing or a curse. On the cloud side, we have cloud-based IAMor identity access management. That is managed by the cloud personnel with the cloud provider. It allows workers and resources to be located anywhere, because if you think about it, they all have the same experience. They're all authorizing to the same cloud-based provider, not trying to go back to the central hub or back to corporate HQ. It may be one experience if you're here, a different experience if you're somewhere else. If it's all done through the cloud, it's the same experience across the board. Then we have optimized policies for onboarding and off-boarding, Cloud providers have a very mature onboarding and off-boarding process and to make sure everybody goes through the same policies and procedures. And then administration, monitoring, and configuration of lifecycle activities are handled by the cloud provider. That in and of itself is a big time saver. You don't have to worry about managing those things in house, so that can take a lot of burden off of your internal personnel and free them up for other things like innovation and actually driving revenue to the business. In summary, we talked about authentication methods and the various technologies associated with that. We talked about smart card authentication, biometrics, the various types, facial, voice, fingerprint, vein analysis, gait analysis. We talked about multi-factor authentication and then also authentication, authorization, and accounting, otherwise known as AAA. Then we finished up with cloud and on-prem requirements as far as authentication is concerned.

BOOK 2

IMPLEMENTING
CYBERSECURITY RESILIENCE

PHYSICAL SECURITY CONTROLS
&
CRYPTOGRAPHIC CONCEPTS

RICHIE MILLER

Introduction

IT Security jobs are on the rise! Small, medium or large size companies are always on the look out to get on board bright individuals to provide their services for Business as Usual (BAU) tasks or deploying new as well as on-going company projects. Most of these jobs requiring you to be on site but since 2020, companies are willing to negotiate with you if you want to work from home (WFH). Yet, to pass the Job interview, you must have experience. Still, if you think about it, all current IT security professionals at some point had no experience whatsoever. The question is; how did they get the job with no experience? Well, the answer is simpler then you think. All you have to do is convince the Hiring Manager that you are keen to learn and adopt new technologies and you have willingness to continuously research on the latest upcoming methods and techniques revolving around IT security. Here is where this book comes into the picture. Why? Well, if you want to become an IT Security professional, this book is for you! If you are studying for CompTIA Security+ or CISSP, this book will help you pass your exam. Passing security exams isn't easy. In fact, due to the raising security beaches around the World, both above mentioned exams are becoming more and more difficult to pass. Whether you want to become an Infrastructure Engineer, IT Security Analyst or any other Cybersecurity Professional, this book (as well as the other books in this series) will certainly help you get there! But, what knowledge are you going to gain from this book? Well, let me share with you briefly the agenda of this book, so you can decide if the following topics are interesting enough to invest your time in! First, you are going to discover how to implement Cybersecurity Resilience. Here, you will learn about redundancy, geographic redundancy, network redundancy, also power and replication redundancy, so that your network can tolerate false outages and bumps. Next we'll cover how to recognize Security Implications of Embedded and Specialized Systems such as SCADA and ICS systems. After that, you will learn about security implications and attack vectors of IoT or Internet of Things devices and specialized systems such as Voice over IP, or VoIP systems. Moving on, you will discover how to secure heating, ventilation, air conditioning, or HVAC systems as well as drones, AVs, and UAVs. We'll also talk about multi-function printers, real-time operating systems, or RTOS, surveillance systems, systems on a chip, communication considerations, and then the constraints we have to deal with when trying to secure all of these systems. Next, you will understand the importance of Physical Security Controls, deterrence as well as digital and logical security on locks, vaults, and sensors. We'll also cover securing infrastructure, such as protected cabling and data access, and then secure disposal of data, such as deleting and the wiping of data. After that, you will discover the Basics of Cryptographic Concepts and you will comprehend digital signatures, the concept of cipher suites, salting and hashing. We'll also go over at a high level quantum communications and quantum computing, blockchain, steganography, and some common use cases, as well as their limitations. If you are ready to get on this journey, let's first cover how to implement Cybersecurity Resilience!

Chapter 1 Geographically Disperse, RAID & Multipath

In the following chapters we'll be talking about Implementing Cybersecurity Resilience. We'll be talking about redundancy and talking about geographic redundancy, network redundancy, also power and replication redundancy, making sure that our networks can tolerate false outages and bumps. Next, we'll be talking about the different types of backups such as incremental and differential backups. We'll be talking about non-persistence, also high availability, the general concept of keeping things highly available, whether it's via power, individual components, storage, networking. We'll also talk about diversity in its various forms, whether it's vendor diversity, technology diversity or crypto. You might ask, what's in it for me, or why should I even care about this? So by putting these things in place, making sure that we're highly available, we can survive outages or bumps, things we that didn't expect to happen, it increases our speed and increases our agility because we're not spending time troubleshooting, we're not spending time on outages, understanding what went wrong and how we could fix it next time because things won't go wrong to begin with, we'll have redundancy or diversity in place, and things to help us mitigate the unexpected. Then if things do happen, we'll understand the different types of backup, taking us back online. Secondly, we'll have a reduction in errors and outages. Those are the types of things that keep you up at night, and a reduction in that is obviously a good thing, and then next, increased resiliency and recoverability. If things happen, if something goes wrong, a piece of equipment fails, a server goes down, if we have increased resiliency and recoverability in place, it allows us to get back online quickly. Then ultimately, all of these things combine to give us peace of mind, and that's where's the name of the game. We want to make sure that we're making our environment as stable as possible and as highly resilient as possible, all the while making sure that our sanity is intact too. Let's dig into the topics that actually make this happen. When we're talking about geographically disperse, what does that mean? What we talked about before, the different types of sites. We have a cold site. It's inexpensive, but long recovery times. We've talked about a warm site, relatively inexpensive. It's cheaper than a hot site, but there is some equipment there, but not everything. There's going to be some time involved to get us actually back up and running. Then we have a hot site, very expensive because we're duplicating everything, bandwidth, power, network, compute storage, you name it. Those things have to be in place so that if we need to failover, we can do so very quickly. Then we have cloud based, or DR as a service, and that's also managed by a provider. It's going to be typically more costly than a cold site or a warm site, but allows us to get up and running quickly, and we don't have to maintain that infrastructure. The cloud provider will have that for us. As we talked about before when we were talking about HA and being out of the way of hurricanes, and having our backup data centers be in different locations so we're not susceptible to hurricanes, well, the same thing here. Let's say, for instance, we have a data center in Florida, as an example, and another one in Georgia, somewhere around Atlanta. Well, those two data centers are fairly geographically dispersed. However, if a hurricane comes through, if they're in the same hurricane path, then they could potentially be hit by the same outage. Whether it's being able to get fuel for backup generators, or a hurricane itself could do damage along a large swath of area, It could span multiple states. A better alternative would be to move that data center somewhere else. If we have the ability to move it even farther out, maybe across the country, that's even better, as long as you don't have geographical mandates that say you have to be "X" amount of miles away due to latency - some applications are very susceptible to latency. The further apart you are, that latency will increase, the round trip time between sites. But depending upon your provider and your connection that may or may not be a problem. But definitely look at geographic dispersal or diversity to improve resiliency and make your applications more resilient and your infrastructure more reliable. Next, let's talk about RAID, and RAID is Redundant Array of Independent or Inexpensive Disks, depending upon where you read, either is correct. It's a fault tolerant array of disks, so data is mirrored or spread across multiple disks and parity is used to recreate the data in the event of a drive failure. If we have an example of RAID 1, the drives here are mirrored. We have Drive 1 and Drive 2, and the blocks of data are mirrored from Drive 1 to Drive 2, They're mirror copies of each other. However, there are many types of RAID, and each provide different levels of protection. As an example, RAID 0. It's important to understand RAID 0, although it says RAID, it is not fault tolerant, so we're just disk striping, so we're spreading the data across multiple disks. But if we lose any one of those disks, we would lose all the data. For fault tolerant, we need to have RAID 1 or better. So RAID 1, is disk mirroring. Then we have RAID 5, which is disk striping with parity. If we have 5 disks in RAID 5 array, it spread across the disks, let's say, for instance, we have A1, A2, A3, and A4, well, what's going to happen is we're going to create a parity stripe based upon the data that's in A1, A2, A3, and A4. We use a parity algorithm that does a mathematical calculation on the data that exists on block A1, A2, A3, and A4. Then it creates a stripe. The next one down, B1, B2, B3, there's now a parity stripe on Disk 4 instead of Disk 5. And then on C, we have the parity stripe on Disk 3, for the D stripe, we have parity on Disk 2, and for the E stripe, we have parity on Disk 1. We never put the parity and the data on the same disk. That way, if a disk fails, we can reconstruct that data. As an example, if Disk 3 fails, well, we have A1, A2, A4, and parity, so we can take A1, 2, and 4, and parity and extrapolate it out and get the data that was A3. For C, as an example, we could do C1, C2, C3, and C4, and then reconstruct the parity stripe, which was missing on Disk 3. Each one of those stripes is able to be reconstructed because we don't have the parity and the data existing on the same disk for each individual stripe. Another one you should be aware of is RAID 6. RAID 6 is disk striping with double parity. And then we have RAID 10, which is disk striping that is mirrored. With RAID 6, we have same 5 disks, but now we have two parity stripes. That gives us the ability to lose 2 disks without losing our data. Just understand the different levels of fault tolerance, the different levels of RAID, which is fault tolerant, which is not, RAID 0 is not, everything else is fault tolerant, and know that these are very much in use today, RAID 5, 6, and 10 being probably the most popular, but these are tried and true methods of fault tolerance. Next, let's talk about the concept of multipath, or multipathing. Multipathing, in simple terms, is a redundancy concept that provides multiple paths, hence the term or hence the name, from point A to point B. It's multiple ways to get to somewhere. That holds true for networking, compute, storage, applications. Multipath will have different connotations, depending upon which context you're using it in, whether it's compute, storage, applications, but generally speaking, let's look at an example here. We have a server, and this server has two HBAs, and an HBA is a host bus adapter. You can think of it like a NIC, or a network interface card, but for a Fibre Channel SAN connectivity, for a SAN, a storage area network, instead of a NIC that would attach to a typical ethernet network. This server has two HBAs, HBA1 and HBA2. They will connect to two different SAN fabrics. Traditionally, in a Fibre Channel network or a storage area network, we have two discrete fabrics that are not connected with each other. That provides for that redundancy. HBA1 and HBA2 will both be connected to each SAN fabric. That way, when it then connects to the actual storage arrays and then the disks on the back end of the storage arrays, the storage array itself may have one or two controllers or multiple controllers, and all of these things, all these different layers of redundancy, add for multipathing. When we make the connectivity and then chase the I/O from server down to the disk, we can see that we may take a specific path. In this case, we see the path here laid out. Well, if that pathway to go down for whatever reason, we could go over a different path and connect to Array Controller 2, or perhaps we may actually go out of HBA2 and connect over SAN Fabric B to Array Controller 2, or if that link is down, over Array Controller 1. You see, it gives us multiple paths from point A to point B, which in turn, as you may guess, gives us that extra layer of redundancy. That way, if there's some issue in the fabric or some issue in collectivity, we can find a different way or a different route to get from server down to the disk itself.

Chapter 2 Load Balancer, Power Resiliency & Replication

A load balancer is a device that will spread the incoming load among multiple pieces of infrastructure, and this deals with servers, storage, and network, and it can provide additional services as well. The term load balancer can be slightly different, depending upon the context that you're using it in. If we look at an example, here, we have a firewall that will sit on the perimeter of our organization, and then we have load balancers that sit behind that firewall, which in turn spread the load across web servers, database servers behind that, and storage behind that. The load balancers are going to, as the name implies, balance the load of the incoming connections that pass through the firewall onto the web servers. We have internal users that can use this as well, but then also external customers that are coming in through the internet. They'll hit through the firewall, their traffic will be load balanced across multiple different connections, multiple different web servers, which will then service customer requests, be it the database, storage. But just understand that load balancers do just as the name implies. They're going to make sure that no single server gets overrun with requests or I/O. Next, we have a few terms around resiliency and power resiliency. Let's talk about uninterruptible power supplies, or a UPS. This is a term you may be familiar with already, and it is typically a battery backup that provides power in the event of a disruption, whether it be a sag, an actual outage, it could be a brownout or a blackout, depending upon the situation. Is it just a dip in current or is it actually completely out? The length of time that these UPSs are actually active and able to supply that backup power depends upon the type of UPS, type of batteries. Next is a generator. A generator is an alternate power supply, typically will run on gas, could be propane, but it would turn itself on if a power dip or outage is detected. Some generators will automatically kick in. Other types of generators need to be flipped over manually. Generally speaking, when we're talking about a data center situation, we're looking at ones that will flip over automatically and kick on as soon as that disruption is identified. When we're talking about dual supply, we're talking about power that is supplied by dual feeds, independent of one another, so we may have an A side and a B side coming into our data center, or to our infrastructure. That way, if one side goes down, has a dip, a brownout, a blackout, we could immediately flip over to the other side, in an active passive, or we may have both sides feeding that infrastructure at the same time, and then we have something referred to as a managed power distribution unit, or a PDU, and that provides the ability to monitor and control critical factors, such as voltage, current, the power factor. These things are typically rack mounted. You'll have them inside the racks, where you have storage, network, compute and they will distribute the power. They can be monitored, they can be smart devices, or they can be just dumb devices that provide power, but we can have situations where we have both A sides and B sides, feed into that PDU, so you don't need two sets of cords going to your infrastructure. They both feed into the PDU, or you may have the load spread across multiple PDUs. Again, depending upon the layer of resiliency that you need. When it comes to resiliency, something else I want to talk about is the concept of replication. Replication, as an example, here we have, let's say, for instance, a West Coast data center, and we have some associated infrastructure. This isn't everything within the data center, but we have firewalls that sit on the outside, we have storage, databases, web servers. Then we also have an East Coast data center, firewalls in the perimeter again.

What we're doing is replicating data from one data center to the other. In that process, we may have actual infrastructure replication like, say, array to array, so we can do replication at the array level, we can do replication at the database level, and we can also do it at the application level. It just depends upon the application that you're running, the criticality of it, is a business critical, is a business necessary. Then what is your actual replication plan? There can be offsite replications, there can be replications within the data center, a four-corners approach, That you have some diversity, like to call it a sprinkler head diversity, That if a sprinkler head were to go off, the replicated data is far enough apart from each other that a single event, like a sprinkler head would not take out all the associated infrastructure, or you can actually replicate offsite, It could be to tape backup for those that are still using tape, it could be to a VTL, and it's replicated out, so we could have data that's stored on the West Coast data center, and then replicated to the East Coast data center. It's certainly not an all-or-nothing approach, so we can have certain pieces of data, but not necessarily the entire thing. We don't need an entire duplicate infrastructure, duplicate number of servers, duplicate amount of storage. You can pick and choose, and replicate just what is necessary. Then, you have another option to replicate to the cloud, so you don't necessarily have to replicate to another data center that you may or may not own, you can also send that data to the cloud, and then restore as necessary. The nice part about that is that you can restore anywhere, assuming you have somewhere to restore to. Next, we have on-prem versus cloud, and on an on-prem situation, we have infrastructure, compute, network, storage. All of that is going to be on-prem. We have duplicate infrastructure, so geo-disperse or four corner redundancy. We also need on-site personnel to manage processes, troubleshoot hardware, also back up and replication software, and then also determining the level of resiliency, the RPO or RTO, the recovery point objective and recovery time objective, and then deciding the data to be backed up and replicated. All of these things are required when we have an on-prem situation. When we're dealing with a cloud, we have infrastructure can be, spun up on-demand, and that's handled by the cloud provider, so we don't necessarily have to have that infrastructure in place ahead of time. It can be spun up elastically, depending upon how things are configured. Also replication will take place between two or more sites, and that's determined by the customer. Then also administration, security, and troubleshooting will be handled by the provider, and you can see a recurring theme here. It takes a lot of the burden off of on-prem sources and puts that on cloud resources or the cloud provider. Also, backups and replication are provided as a service, so as you're instantiating your services, applications or databases, typically it's more or less a checkbox within the configuration settings to back this information up. The backup and replication is provided more or less as a service. You'll still determine the level of resiliency, the RPO and RTO, and then what data to be backed up and replicated, that's not going to change, you still have control, and you have to make the decision over what is actually replicated.

Chapter 3 Backup Execution Policies

When talking about backup plans, what we need to be concerned with is what data needs to be backed up? What's the retention policy? Is it the same for all data? Because at the end of the day, not all data actually needs to be backed up. Some of it's not that important, some of it needs to be highly available, some of it needs to be retrievable at a moments notice, other data could be carted off to some type of cold storage, and there's varying degrees in between. Not everything has to be backed up at the same rate or even backed up it all. We need to make sure we define these things ahead of time and understand what the retention policy is for that data, and is it the same for all data? But, what's the RPO and the RTO? The recovery point objective and the recovery time objective. Then, additionally, where do the backups actually live? Are they on-array? Are they off-array? Are they in disk, or VTL, a virtual tape library, or on tape? Or they backed up off site? Each of these options have different costs associated with them, also varying amounts of speed, reliability. So depending upon the budget, how much data needs to be backed up, and how quickly it needs to be recovered will dictate to some degree where those back apps actually live. When it comes to backup execution and frequency, some things to consider are the Recovery Point Objective, or the RPO, and the Recovery Time Objective, or the RTO. So, how often do backups occur, and how quickly does the data need to be recovered? You should have SLAs, or Service Level Agreements, in place defined for these things. Also, how long should that data be retained? Next, we need to ensure that backups can occur actually within the backup window, as per the SLA, or the Service Level Agreement. A couple questions to ask there, do the backups that we have planned, do they conflict with other backups taking place? In a small environment, you may have only a few backups per day, or maybe a couple dozen. In a large environment, you may have literally thousands of backup jobs taking place each and every day. It's very important to understand what conflicts, and does that impact my SLA? Secondly, do these backups impact server performance or network performance? There's a good chance that it might, depending on how it's architected. Those backups might need to take place off hours, or whatever is defined as a slow period within your organization. Some companies will have actually separate backup networks so that it doesn't impact normal network and normal server traffic, but again, it depends upon your organization and how things are architected. All of these things need to be discovered, documented, and defined ahead of time. Let's now talk about backup concepts. There's several backup types that I want you to be familiar with. The first is differential. A differential backup is data that has changed since the last full backup. The key takeaway here is the time to backup increases over time because each day we're adding what's changed since the last full backup. Let's say we did a full backup on Sunday. Monday, not much has changed. We do a very quick differential backup. Tuesday, some more stuff has changed, so that differential now takes a little longer. Wednesday, Thursday, and so on. That will increase each day because the amount of data between the differential and the last full backup will increase. The time to backup increases over time, but the time to restore is reduced, and it only requires two backup media, the last differential and the last full backup. Those two will get you back to where you need to be. Next we have incremental backups. An incremental is data that's changed since the last incremental backup. The time to backup is reduced, but the time to restore is increased - it's the reverse. And this is because all incremental backups are required, plus the last full backup. Each day when you do that incremental, all you're capturing is the stuff that's changed since the last incremental. If we did a last full backup on Sunday and then we did an incremental Monday, Tuesday, Wednesday, Thursday, outage occurs on Friday, we're going to need all the incremental Monday through Thursday, plus the last full backup. Then we have, which is, as the name implies, all data is backed up each time. It takes the longest amount of time to back up and restore, but you capture everything at once. Then we have something referred to as a snapshot. Now, a snapshot is a point in time copy of that data, just like if you took a picture; hence, the term snapshot. What happens here is that snapshot will typically maintain pointers to the original data, rather than actually copying the data itself. It keeps track of what's changed, and those pointers allow very quick backups. You could take a snapshot literally in seconds, depending upon what type of media it's sitting on, spinning disk versus flash media. If you look at incremental versus differential, you'll see an incremental backup schedule. Here we have a backup type of incremental. Sunday we're going to do a full backup. Monday is incremental - any changes since Sunday. Tuesday, Wednesday, you can see, each day we're doing incremental backups, but what we're capturing is only the changes since the previous day. It's incrementally building upon itself. We're capturing those incremental changes. Well, if we need to restore, let's say, for instance, we need to restore on Saturday, we have to restore the last full backup, plus all the incremental. All the incremental from Monday, Tuesday, Wednesday, Thursday, Friday, Conversely, if we're doing a differential backup, well, you can see the same thing. We're going to take a backup, a full backup, rather, on Sunday, and then on Monday, we'll do a differential. That's only the changes since Sunday. On Tuesday, we do another differential. Well, guess what? All the changes since Sunday. On Wednesday, Thursday, Friday, et cetera, each time we do that differential backup, it's capturing all the changes since the last full backup. As you can imagine, the size of those differentials will increase each day, but then when it comes time to restore, let's say, for instance again, we had a crisis on Saturday, all we have to restore is the last differential, plus the full backup, it makes restoral much quicker. Let's now talk about the concept of backup environments and different ways we can get these backups accomplished. Let's say, for instance, we have a server sitting in our data center. We have two different choices, really, for connecting that to some type of attached storage. We have Network Attached Storage, or NAS, and we also have SAN, or a Storage Area Network. One is file-based, one is blocked-based. A NAS device will be presented to the server as a NAS share, whereas SAN storage is presented to the server and it looks like a local disk. That's the two different main environments. From there, on the NAS side, we could replicate that data from the NAS device to another NAS device. So, that's replication at the array level. Similarly, for SAN, we could also replicate to another SAN array. That goes back to what I was saying previously, where we could replicate at the array level. From there, we also have some additional choices. We could replicate to a tape library or back up to a tape library, or we could also back up to cloud. Along those same lines, we can do the same thing from a SAN array, back up to tape or back up to cloud. Although it's not drawn here specifically, typically, there'll be an agent that's installed on the server, and the backup will take place from the server directly, either out to tape or out to cloud. Or, we can, replicate the NAS device or the SAN device to make sure the data remains accessible. When we talk about online versus offline backups, let's say, for instance, we have a main data center, we have a lot of disks, we have a lot of information, critical information, business critical, business necessary. Well, we want to protect that data against some type of an event, whether it's a malware attack or ransomware attack. One methodology would be the concept of a cyber bunker. In a cyber bunker, what we do is we replicate a subset or potentially all, but typically a subset of our main data, we're going to identify our business critical applications, we'll replicate that data over to that cyber bunker, but the replication link only remains up while the replication takes place. In other words, we error gap that connection. The connection comes up, in other words, we turn on the ports between the two data centers only when that replication takes place. As soon as the replication is done, that link gets severed. That way, if an attacker gets into our network, they can't bridge that gap, they can't bridge that connection from the main data center to the cyber bunker and potentially infect our backups We're going to make sure those backups remain in an immutable form, tucked away from our main data, and then we may have some additional resources within the cyber bunker to do forensic analysis and help us remediate in the event of a situation, but the main concept is the cyber bunker is going to be typically a subset of our main data, it's going to be logically error gapped That it's only up while their application takes place, and then once their application is done, the link is severed. A few things to consider when we're talking about backups, specifically, around distance considerations, so backups versus high availability, backups could be geographically far away, and that can be asynchronous versus high availability, or HA, which requires synchronous speeds. What I mean by that is the placement of our backup infrastructure needs to be consistent with our idea of what we're actually accomplishing. Backups can be far away because we're not doing it in real time in asynchronous fashion. High availability, however, has to be electronically close enough so the round trip time between those two sites is small enough, that latency is low enough, so that we can do synchronous replication or even write to both locations at the same time. Next, the physical backup distance limitations. If we are backing up the tape, as an example, how long would it take to get the tapes back in the event of a disaster? There's no right answer to this one, but it's a matter of understanding realistically those timelines and those time frames. When you're doing your business continuity or your disaster recovery planning, you factor those times into your restore process. It takes 3 or 4 hours to even get the tapes on site, and it takes another 3 or 4 hours or maybe a day or 2 to restore, all of those things should be calculated into your assessment. Then recovery testing, whether it's a hot site, a warm site, cold site, the time required to recover the offsite backups, the order of recovery, that's another big one that needs to be documented to make sure we understand exactly the order of restoration because you can't necessarily restore everything at once. It has to be a specific order sometimes, application, database, middleware. Then also, are the backups that we're doing app consistent or crash consistent? All of these things have to be tested, and they should be tested as realistically as possible, whatever your business allows for, maybe once a quarter, perhaps once a year, but they should actually be tested That you don't find that out in the middle of an actual crisis that, uh, oh, our actual backups aren't even there, or they don't work, or the stuff we recovered is not actually usable because it's not in the state that can be used by the application. All of these things are critical to make sure that the recovery process is successful.

A few other concepts we need to cover that I want you to be familiar with and the first is non-persistence. Non-persistence prevents people from customizing their desktops, installing unapproved applications, tweaking settings. This is typically associated with things like VDI, virtual desktop infrastructure. We may provide desktops as an example in a VDI instance, or contractors for developers, call center agents, things along those lines, and we don't want them to be able to necessarily tweak things, to make things more difficult to configure, troubleshoot, maintain. Every time they log off, anything that was changed while that user had that session open or that VDI session open, gets lost. Next time they boot up, they're back to a clean state. So preventing them from installing or tweaking things reduces troubleshooting and prevents unauthorized installation of applications. Next, we have snapshots. Snapshots allow a user to quickly revert to a known good state or roll back changes in the event of a virus, a malware incident, spyware. Two concepts there come two rolled into one. A snapshot allows us to roll back to a known good state. We can physically take a snapshot, and some operating systems will do this behind the scenes as we install drivers. Windows as an example, will create a last known good configuration. If something doesn't quite turn out we have an issue, we can revert back to a last known good configuration. Also, if we're in the middle of say a maintenance upgrade, we're doing some things overnight, maybe doing a maintenance window, if we have an issue, we can roll back that change to get us back to that last known good state. Then we have live boot media. This concept allows for a fully operational operating system, or an OS, either on a USB drive or some type of removable media that allows the cleaning of a system, removing of malware, or you could run the operating system from that removable media for however long. It's not the optimal way to do it. You don't want to do that every single time, but it does allow you to boot up a machine off of that USB drivers and do what you need to do. Those things work well when you need to boot up outside of the actual disk that's in the computer and then use the live boot media to clean it, remove malware, spyware.

Chapter 4 High Availability, Redundancy & Fault Tolerance

Our next concept is high availability. This is two or more systems that are in sync at or near real time. We're split writing, if you will. We're writing two systems at one time or very close to real time. We can failover between systems and minimize disruption. For example, we have one site, Site A, it's comprised of some ESXi infrastructure, a couple of VMs running, some servers, we have some virtualization infrastructure as well for our SAN, VPLEX in this example. But, we can also set up another site, in this case, Site B. That way, we have the ability to VMotion between sites, we have a VMotion network between our clusters, we have a distributed mirrored volume between our VPLEXs, and then we have SAN arrays in both locations. In essence, we're writing to both locations. They're going to synchronize pretty much in real time. That's dependent upon how far away they are. If there's more than, say, 5 or 10 milliseconds of latency between the sites, it can, depending upon the application and it's tolerance for latency, that may not be feasible. But if the applications and the data centers are close enough, then you can do in real time, have that synchronous replication and make sure you have availability in both sites. For high availability, backup data centers need to be relatively close, roughly 30 to 50 miles away, if possible, low latency between locations to ensure synchronous replication of data. You don't want one on the East Coast and one of the West Coast and expect synchronous replication. Also, do I need assessment? What systems and applications actually need HA? Not all do. Also, what systems and applications need offsite DR, or disaster recovery? Because there is a differentiation between the two. A needs assessment of that specific site and the applications within that site are really what's necessary to determine because you're not going to want to do this for every single application. It's very costly because it's not really just bunkering the data from one site to the other. You're going to need all the infrastructure as well, the servers, the applications, the understanding of which order they need to be brought up in right. There's a lot of work that goes in behind the scenes to make sure this is done properly, but it's crucial for business critical applications. Because even though it's a high cost associated with these types of solutions, what is the cost of that critical application goes down? If you're making whatever, a million dollars an hour or $3 million a minute, whatever the case might be, how much does that downtime cost versus what's the cost of a synchronous replication or a high availability site close by? Along those same lines we have redundancy. Redundancy covers all areas of an application stack, so redundant servers, power supplies, RAID, NICs, HBAs. We're also talking about networking switches and fabrics and storage arrays. If you want true redundancy, and you want to say your application is redundant, well, it's not just the application, it's not just the server, all of the things that make up that stack need to be redundant as well so there is no single point of failure, so servers, power supplies, and so on. We need to make sure that if any one of those things goes down, it does not have the ability to take that specific application offline. Another way to do that is also with clustering, multiple servers operating as one. It could be MS SQL Server, it could be Oracle RAC, also hot spares. Data is copied over proactively, so a hot spare in a storage array, as an example, is a mechanism that can detect when a drive is about to fail. You're going to have spare drives in the array already, or in the server. Those drives sit there and they're not used until something starts to go bad, and The data would then be proactively copied over from the failing drives over to those hot spares, and then you either dispatch a technician to go out and swap those drives out and replace them with good drives, and then they become the new hot spares. Something else to keep in mind is the fact that that spare can be a dedicated disk or it can be space on multiple disks, so it doesn't necessarily have to be a disk all by itself. Instead of having a hot spare you could have hot space, That things are copied over to whatever space is available on those drives, and then bad space or the bad blocks on that disk are marked as such That no new data is copied over to those locations. When we're talking about hardware, fault tolerant hardware means having redundant components in case one fails so that operations can continue. Much like I just talked about at the entire stack level, now we're talking about the individual hardware component level. In this instance, we have disks, the networking cards, NICs or the HBAs, the power supplies, the fans. It's a storage array, the storage processors, the engines and the directors. All of these things need to be redundant. As an example, we have multiple servers, we have our fault tolerant network. If we start to see where something actually starts to go south, you can see the middle server, we could remotion those instances or those workloads off of the failing server onto either one of the good servers without any disruption to the business. That can't happen if we don't have redundant components inside as well. Next, let's talk about the concept of diversity. What I mean by diversity is diversity of technologies, vendors, cryptographic keys, security controls. Let's take a look at each of these individually. When we're talking about technology diversity, why do we do that? What's the point? While technology diversity is the concept of using more than one type of technology to accomplish a given task, that safeguards against things like bugs or vulnerabilities that may otherwise take down an entire system. In essence, you can think of it as not a single point of failure. It provides a method of failback and failover also in the event of an incident. We have multiple technologies we can utilize. If one doesn't work, we can either failover to the other or quickly instantiate that other technology to bring it online very quickly. Next we have vendor diversity. Vendor diversity helps safeguard against things like supply chain attacks and incidents. If we have more than one vendor that we're dealing with, that way, if one gets compromised or is not available, we have others that we can choose from. It provides vendor lock-in, so we're not tied to a specific vendor. If one is either not available or doesn't have something that we need, we can obviously choose from another vendor. Then, realistically, it gives us more financial leverage. If we have multiple vendors to choose from, then no one vendor realizes they have all of our eggs in one basket, so we can leverage or pit one against the other. In essence, the business risk of having all of our systems, our data, technology, and/or knowledge in the hands of a single vendor introduces, to some extent, a level of risk. By spreading that out across multiple vendors, we mitigate that to a degree. Next, we have crypto and control diversity. With crypto diversity, we would rotate cryptographic keys and also use technologies from more than one provider. If there's bugs, or if one is compromised, we have multiples that we can choose from, and we're not completely dependent on one technology to provide that solution. Same thing with controls diversity - Diversification ensures overlap. It also provides wider coverage. Let's take a look at that one in more detail. Antivirus, threat detection, ransomware prevention - all of these things should be following a defense in depth methodology - layered technologies. When we're talking about layered technologies, we don't necessarily want three or four different technologies that do exactly the same thing. As an example, if we have technology A. Let's say the technology A has a 75% success rate for antivirus or threat detection, ransomware protection. Technology A, hey, we're going to diversify. Let's go ahead and buy technology B. That also has a 75% success rate. Well, that's great, but we need to follow defense in depth, so let's go out and buy technology C. Well, if all three of those have the same 75% success rate, meaning they all pretty much correlate with one another, and they all find or address the same exact issues, but what happens is, we have very little overlap, That gives us a 75% success rate, but also a 25% failure rate. If those three technologies are not tightly correlated, well, then we can see, we start to spread out a little bit more and our risk goes down, because now we have three different technologies that aren't exactly similar. Something that technology A may not cover, technology B might find, or technology C might find. The less correlated they are, as we see, it becomes more spread out, then our coverage increases. Having multiple technologies is great as long as they're not identical of each other, and it seems counterintuitive, but the less correlated they are with each other, it actually spreads our coverage wider and gives us a better chance of picking up those threats, antivirus and ransomware. In summary we talked about redundancy. We talked about geographic redundancy, network redundancy, things like power and also replication redundancy. We talked about the various backup types. We talked about non-persistence, and what that means as far as recoverability, and making our data available. We talked about high availability and how that works, along with diversity, whether it's vendor, technology, controls, cryptographic technologies.

Chapter 5 Embedded Systems & SCADA Security

In the following chapters, we'll be covering Recognizing Security Implications of Embedded and Specialized Systems. We're going to start off with embedded systems, and we'll talk about SCADA systems and ICS systems. We'll talk more about what they mean and the security implications. We'll talk about the Internet of Things and how massively that's growing, and also the attack vector is growing right along with it. We'll talk about specialized systems, also Voice over IP, or VoIP systems. We talk about heating, ventilation, and air conditioning, or HVAC. We also talk about drones and AVs, and also, UAVs. We'll talk about multi-function printers, also, real-time operating systems, or RTOS. We'll talk about surveillance systems, systems on a chip, communication considerations, and then the constraints we have to deal with when trying to secure all of these systems. The main goal here is that embedded systems, they're literally everywhere. They control things from thermostats to critical infrastructure. What I want you to do is think about from a security mindset is to just realize that really everything is a target. Be aware of all the things that are around you in your environment, things you may take for granted. Obviously, the big things that everyone thinks about, router, switches, or infrastructure servers, storage, all of those things, or the main components that make up our network and make up our infrastructure are natural things to focus on. But the other things, too, the wearables, the IoT devices - all of these things become attack vectors and attack services. There are ways for hackers to get their foot in the door. As we know, once their foot is in the door, they elevate privileges, they install persistence, they maintain persistence, they can come and go as they please, they pivot, once they're inside of our network, jump from network to network and explore. They extract things of value, or they destroy, or they just sit there and wait. Different groups have different methods of operation and different goals. Some are easy to detect, some are difficult. The easiest way to avoid all of that, is to not let them in in the first place. The thing that compounds that, obviously, is the fact that these things can leave our environment, go outside of our perimeter, go outside of our safety zones, and then come back into our network. It used to be that laptops were the primary culprit for that. But now with wearables and IoT devices, things can come and go much more easily. To start off, let's talk about what actually is an embedded system. An embedded system is a microprocessor-based computer hardware system with software that is designed to perform a very specific or a dedicated function, either as an independent system or as part of a larger system. The core of this is an integrated circuit, or an IC, that's designed to carry out computation for real-time operations. These embedded systems are very scaled down. They're not like regular computers that we think of, like a laptop or desktop. They're not designed to do everything well. They're designed to do very specific functions with very low latency and to process things in pretty much real time. They don't do a lot of things good. They do one or two things very well and very rapidly. They have embedded systems for very specific functions, There's a different type of embedded system for different types of utilities, different types of functions, different pieces of equipment, different industries. When it comes to embedded systems, a few that I want you to be familiar with; we have one called Raspberry Pi; you may have heard of that before. A Raspberry Pi is actually a fully functional computer; CPU, Wi-Fi, Bluetooth, video, not a video card, but onboard integrated video, and it's also expandable.

These small devices can be embedded in a number of different pieces of hardware and can run a myriad of applications. In essence, you could connect a monitor, keyboard and actually use this as a fully functioning computer. Next, we have a field programmable gate array, or an FPGA, not to be confused with a flip chip pin grid array, also known as an FPGA, totally different thing. In this instance, we're talking about a field programmable gate array, and this is an integrated circuit designed to be configured or programmed after manufacturing. All of the circuitry are building blocks inside of the ICs that can be configured or programmed after it's built, so you buy it, it's a blank slate, and you can program it to your needs. Next, we have something referred to as an Arduino. an Arduino, at first pass, may look similar to a Raspberry Pi, but they're very different. An Arduino device is a single board microcontroller versus having a microprocessor. A microcontroller is used for very specific functions. Think of it almost like an embedded system we talked about before. It's not a general purpose computer, but they're designed for very specific functions. These types of things, as well, are stackable. The pins and the pin slots on this board, and it's designed to be stacked, so you can have different functions added onto, and there's a number of different ones that can be added and give it additional capabilities, but these things are designed for very specific functions. Some things need to be concerned with. When we're talking about SCADA, or supervisory control and data acquisition, you may or may not be familiar with that term, but it's very important that you understand what it is and the implications if these things are not maintained properly, it has a big impact or a big potential impact because these types of systems usually refer to a centralized system that which monitor and control entire sites or complexes of systems spread throughout large areas. What does that really mean? Well think about water treatment facilities, the electrical grid, the power grid, things along those lines that really encompass large areas of critical infrastructure. We have such things as an RTU, or a remote terminal unit, and that is connections to sensors, and it's going to convert that sensor information, and whatever that sensor might be, whether it's on a pipe or some piece of equipment within a larger system, that needs to give off sensors, and alerts, they might check the temperature, or the pressure, or the amount of electricity, or voltage. There's going to be a sensor connected to that. The RTU then converts that sensor information into digital data. Next is a programmable logic unit, or a logic controller, rather, a PLC. It's similar to an RTU, but PLCs are a little newer, they're more versatile, more economical, but they do the same type of function. They're going to report into a master terminal unit, or MTU. Next we have a human machine interface, an HMI, and that's going to present the data that's collected from these RTUs or PLCs to a human operator who can then act upon that specific data. They may need to adjust valves or make sure that things are within acceptable ranges. Then master terminal unit, or the MTU, is what sends information and instructions to the RTU or the PLC. And it's also going to receive instructions back and aggregate all that information. In a SCADA environment you may have some type of master control area, or like a control center, where you have all the different screens from your different systems, whether it's a nuclear power plant, or a water treatment facility, or an electrical grid, sewage system. These PLCs and RTUs are spread out throughout the entire system. They all report back to the MTU, and you have an operator that sits there and manages, and maintains, and monitors all these things. If we look at this in a little more detail, in a SCADA system we have the RTUs, they're going to be computers set up along the network, and typically these are closed off networks that are not connected to the internet, least traditionally. You'll see as we go along here, they've evolved from a non-connected air gapped system into things that are now more distributed networked or actually connected to the internet. But at any rate, we have the RTUs that are connected to our network, they all report into an MTU, we have a human interface that actually looks in and controls, and then we have people that have access potentially through the internet, it just depends. In this type of an environment, we have to be aware of the fact that we could have a remote access hacker that could get in if our machine, or network is connected to the internet, or if we have some type of access point, whether it is a legitimate access point or a rogue access point, we may have a remote access attacker who can come in with from within our network, even if it's not connected to the internet per se, if they're able to get access to the network itself, they could potentially do some harm. As you can imagine, these things are very widespread. They connect and control large pieces of infrastructure, so we want to make sure that we have these things as secure as possible. One way we may do that, let's just say, for instance, all of our SCADA systems, these terminals cannot be updated, they're just in a situation where they are what they are, we can't patch them. We wouldn't be able to apply, let's say, for instance, a host-based intrusion detection system. We wouldn't be able to put anything on the host specifically, but we could put a network-based intrusion detection system. We could firewall off the network itself, and then we could put some type of network intrusion detection system in place, so that if any type of attacker were to come in remotely or even if they're attaching to the network itself, we could detect that intrusion. We also have to discuss some SCADA security concerns. When these types of systems were first invented and first brought online, they were very monolithic. They were not connected to the internet, and they weren't really designed to be connected to anything else. They were just very self-contained systems. Security wasn't really as much of an issue as it is today. It wasn't really baked in and as big of a concern. For the monolithic, it's evolved into a distributed system, which has then evolved into networked, and you can see the progression here. From networked and then we now went into the Internet of Things, and we have access potentially from anywhere. Some security implications and some concerns would be unauthorized access, whether it be malware, viruses, we could have hacking attempts and theft or destruction of data, or at the very least, to plant something that's going to allow them to have a back door at some later point. All of these things are big concerns from a security standpoint. We also have to understand that these types of attacks can be used to degrade or destroy critical infrastructure. Two big examples; one you may or may not be aware of, the other was all over the news for many, many months and actually a couple of years now, but in 2000 in Australia, there was a sewage system that was attacked. It ended up being a disgruntled internal employee, but that person was able to in effect, shut down the sewage system and it backed up throughout parks and throughout all areas within Australia or a lot of areas within Australia. In 2010, a much more determined and a much more focused attack that was actually using code as a weapon. It was a very specific attack by either the US and Israel, but it was created as a weapon, and it was targeted specifically at the PLCs and the SCADA systems that were used in Iran's nuclear facilities by inserting malware. There was an air-gapped system, but it was on USB drives that somebody apparently had plugged in, and when they went into that specific system, it infected and downloaded some vulnerabilities and they were able to find out exactly what PLCs they needed to attack. As soon as they found out that the one that it needed, it was able to destroy up to a fifth of the centrifuges within that nuclear facility, causing the centrifuges to spin out of control. The implication of that is, or the scary part is, the malware or the actual attack reported back to the HMIs, the human machine interface, and reported back to the operators, that everything was fine. They had no idea that the centrifuges were spinning out of control until it was too late. They burned themselves out and were destroyed. It severely crippled Iran's nuclear facilities during that time period. SCADA systems have obviously great use, they have a lot of potential, but they also have a huge potential for impact if they're breached. We rely heavily on these types of things for critical infrastructure throughout pretty much all facets of society.

Chapter 6 Smart Devices / IoT & Special Purpose Devices

When it comes to smart devices, or internet of things or IoT devices, we have to cover a few things. Wearable technology is becoming more and more pervasive everywhere, as far as watches, heart monitors, fitness devices, and there's more coming. Every time you turn around, there's some new device, or some new use case; always connected, continuously feeding information about location, our habits, our health so that increases the attack vector, making interception of data easier. If you think about it, a potential concern would be, if a hacker is able to access all this data, they could, number one, compromise the data, use it for social engineering purposes; they could even sell that data, potentially, to companies that are not necessarily on the up and up, that could use that data against you for monetary gain. They could use it for social engineering, where they could go out and now develop a more complete profile of who you are and what you do, what you like. If they were to launch some type of email scam or spear phishing campaign and they were able to use your specific data, that's personal to you, it becomes much more credible to the person they're trying to contact, perhaps a friend, or an associate of yours. Next, we have home automation. Along the same lines, same thought process, that personal data can be compromised. Entry points into a user's network, and ultimately, really their life, when you think about it. Social engineering becomes even easier. The more a hacker knows, as we talked about, and again, these are all attack vectors. These are threat vectors. The attack surface starts to spread, even though they're in tiny devices that you don't necessarily think about. They have embedded systems that should be patched, firmware updates just like any other computer system, or operating system. A lot of times, these things don't have either the capability to do that, or you don't think about doing it. Well, all of those things now become a way into the network. If someone's able to hack a device, and that device connects to your home network, they can get into your network just like they would in a corporate environment. If they're able to get in, elevate privileges, pivot, jump onto perhaps, you bring your work laptop home; now they're into your personal network. They're able to use that to get into a work laptop. You take that into the office. That malware still exists. If they were able to get in and establish a persistent connection, that's another possible way into a corporate enterprise, or a corporate network. All of these things start to compound on each other and makes it even more critical that we maintain and monitor and update or patch. Now, just to reiterate for smart devices and IoT things, so as you mentioned, sensors, wearables, smart devices, facility automation devices, all of these things can make life more convenient and also more real-time interactivity, easier to manage. But as we talked about, they also increase a company's attack surface. What we need to make sure that we do is we don't allow weak defaults. Most of these things have known vulnerabilities and weak defaults, like default passwords. It's very important to change these default passwords and settings and also routinely audit the environment to understand what IoT devices exist on the network and what types of data they actually transmit and also to where. We need to make sure that we have a good understanding of what is on our network, and it's not a once and done, nor is it a set it and forget it type of process. We need to make sure we do these things with some type of regular cadence, whether it's once a quarter, once a year, every six months. It's going to apply differently for each organization, but auditing to make sure we understand what is on the network is critical. Next, we have special purpose devices. The first one up is medical devices. Medical devices pose a risk on multiple levels. They can be hacked and adversely affect a person's health, they can obviously produce a massive amount of data, that data can be used against that person, or it can be used to formulate some type of social engineering component or sold to other companies, data mined, and these devices often contain embedded systems that are not routinely patched and updated. An interesting fact is that hospitals typically have 3X to 4X. There are 300 or 400% more medical devices than they do IT equipment. If these devices aren't patched and maintained, just like we do everything else, that's a huge potential risk for compromise and for breach. Just like the 2014 NIST voluntary framework assessment, the NIST guidelines we talked about previously, the same cybersecurity policies we apply to our traditional networks should be applied to the medical devices and the IoT devices that serve up the medical and the health-related fields. Next we have motor vehicles, and as you can imagine, as these things become more and more technologically advanced, and they become connected to the internet, they can be compromised just like anything else. There's potential for sabotage or vehicle impairment, theft of customer data, again, these types of devices produce lots and lots of data continuously, telemetry information, where you're going and when, your speed your routines - all of these things could be used to go to profile against you. Also disruption in services, we can shut the car down. If a hacker successfully exploits something in the vehicle, and someone gets injured or some type of monetary damage occurs, well, there you have reputational damages, and also consumer confidence. That has an impact to a company's bottom line, investors. Getting back to the sabotage and vehicle impairment, it was a hack of a Chrysler Jeep vehicle back in 2015, and the short of it is security researchers, this was more of a controlled demo of possibilities, but these security researchers were able to hack the Jeep and commanding it to drive into a ditch. That is not good, I mean, it goes without saying. Imagine driving down the road and all of a sudden your car just takes over, and it drives where it wants to. Especially with the more autonomous cars coming down the pike, it's a great feature that's going to ultimately save a lot of lives, but hackers are always going neck and neck, the good guys and the bad guys are constantly battling to try to outsmart and out do each other. Just like any other industry, there's constant vigilance that needs to be applied to make sure these devices are secure as possible. Next, let's talk about Voice over IP, or VoIP. VoIP has actually been around since the mid 1990s. It's been around for quite a while, it's a mature technology. Many companies have switched from traditional PSTN or public switched telephone networks, which are circuit based, to modern VoIP systems, which are packet switched and traverse over the Internet. PBX systems everyone is switching from those older systems to Voice over IP systems. Voice over IP is actually a suite of protocols, and we won't dig into that too, too much. It's beyond the scope of what we're going to talk about here, but it's a suite of protocols, including MGCP, which is a Media Gateway Control Protocol or a connection management for media gateways, also SIP or Session Initiation Protocol, and the older H.323 protocol, which was introduced when VoIP first came out. It allows, as you might guess, voice and video calling over IP networks, in other words, the internet. A few VoIP concerns, however, since we're dealing with IP traffic, IP packets traversing over an IP network of the internet. We have very much the same concerns that we would have with any host connected to the internet. Eavesdropping, vishing, which is Voice over IP phishing. Well, same process, just using VoIP as the communication medium. Also, viruses and malware. Just like we have with a host on a network, viruses and malware can also be introduced here as well. Denial-of-service attacks, something called SPIT, or Spamming over Internet Telephony. We're spamming, just like we would on an email platform, we have the potential to compromise the system, and just like we would send out millions of emails, we can send out millions of bogus phone calls using a robo-dialer or some type of mechanism; it's just an new IP address on the other side of the connection. We can do a similarly annoying and very frustrating process of spam over the VoIP network instead of our traditional method. Then call tampering and also on-path attacks, formerly Man-in-the-Middle attacks, very similar to an on-path attack when a host is attaching to a server or a web server.

Chapter 7 HVAC, Aircraft/UAV & MFDs

Next, we have HVAC systems. Heating, ventilating, and air condition systems provide, as you might guess, proper temperature control, humidity control. Excessive heat can wreak havoc on electronic devices. The heat itself can cause something to overheat, or if we start messing with the HVAC and turning it up and down and perhaps creating condensation, we can create condensation, which equals water which is bad for electronics. A hacker, a skilled hacker, could go in and manipulate that HVAC system to affect computers, networking or storage. All of these things can wreak havoc on electronic devices and the networks in general. It becomes a target. If someone wants to take down a specific entity, a data center, or a company, in general, they can do so potentially by manipulating these types of networks. It's not just the computer systems - there's the ancillary systems that all make up this attack surface, and I keep using that word. It's the global picture. You have to look at the entire landscape and say, what are all the different ways that someone can get into my network? What are all the different ways someone can get access to my data or negatively affect or negatively impact my company. As an IT professional, as a security professional, we need to be looking at all of these different avenues of attack and making sure that we're protecting against them, we're monitoring, updating, patching, and shoring up our defenses using layered defenses, making sure we have multiple layers of defense for a hacker to have to get through before they get access to our corporate or proprietary data. Some HVAC areas of concern, proper humidity needs to be maintained. Low humidity can create static electricity. Static electricity is not good. A lot of electronic equipment, a lot of the circuitry inside of a computer runs on 5 volts or 12 volts, or even less. Well, if you have static electricity, if someone were to go across the carpet and have enough static electricity to actually generate a spark when they go to touch something, that could be upwards of 30,000 volts. That spark that just gives you a little bit of a bite and, jumps from your finger to whatever you're touching may not seem like a big deal, but that is enough to fry a piece of electronic circuitry on a server or a network switch or something like that. If that happens, that could potentially take down a piece of your fabric, or your network, or a critical component to an application, or so forth. It has the potential to be severely impacting. Conversely, high humidity can create condensation or moisture. Moisture is not good for electronic components. Collectively, an entire data center can be compromised if the HVAC system is purposely degraded or destroyed. These are one of those systems that we need to closely monitor. Next, we have aircraft and unmanned aircraft, or UAVs. Unmanned aircraft, just like we talked about with cars, can be compromised. Hackers, terrorists can have access, organized crime, the same types of groups that would attack a traditional computer network can do the same thing with these types of devices. Now, the scary part, or where it becomes a big area of concern, is if they're compromised, these types of devices can be weaponized to deliver ammunitions, they can drop bombs, that could crash into things, or they could be used to spy on ourselves. If a terrorist group took control of a drone, they could actually take the feed from that drone, they could spy on troop movements, ammunitions, deployments. It's especially important in military and government application that these things are highly secured, and there is a whole different level of encryption. But there are a ton of consumer-grade devices that can also be used for these same types of purposes. A bad actor could take control or intercept communications. They could disperse weapons, they could spy or snoop on targets. They can also do something called GPS spoofing, and they pony up false GPS coordinates, so the drone thinks it's somewhere else. It thinks it's in a different place than it is, it's a different time, it's a different speed. The hacker could then take control of that drone and direct it wherever they want it to go. All of the things that are created to make our lives easier to give us additional capabilities can also be used against us. It's very, very important that IT security, or cybersecurity in general, really ramps up and apply themselves to these areas specifically. Encryption is still our best line of defense, so encrypted GPS mitigates that threat. If it's encrypted, they're not able to take control and offer up false coordinates. All the military grade or government grade drones and unmanned aircraft they have that already in place. Consumer grade, though, typically doesn't, or it's not as strong, which still gives the bad actor the ability to use these devices against us. Next, when it comes to printers and multifunction devices, printers and MFDs can contain very sensitive information. People print very sensitive data from time to time, they'll copy things, so all of these things get stored on a hard drive in that system, potentially. All of these things need to be patched and updated regularly. This is a very systematic approach to IT security, we need to patch and update regularly. Especially as the network and the size of the company grows and scales, that patching becomes more and more of a challenge, especially when you have a lot of different systems, Linux and Windows variations and different flavors of OSs, all of those things have to be updated on a specific cadence. When it comes to printers, again, patch update regularly, also, use static IP addresses when possible. That alleviates the DNS cache poisoning potential, direct that prints queue somewhere else, potentially compromise that data. Next, we have firewalls. We need to make sure these things are in place and functioning properly. Also, we have access control. Who's actually logging into these things? Who's actually using the devices to copy or scan. If we have one set of credentials that everyone uses, it's going to be very, very difficult, if not impossible, for us to then go back and audit if we have to do some type of forensic procedures, some type of forensic accounting of who is doing what. If everyone's using the same account, we can't do that. Credentials access control is very important, and also, centralized printer pools. That way, we have one place to essentially manage, and audit, and update. Then also we have hard drive encryption where possible. Just like with any other system, we want to use encryption whenever possible to maintain an additional layer of security. That way, if someone grabs that printer or that MFD, puts it over their shoulder, and walks out of the data center or walks out of the office, that hard drive is encrypted. The data on that hard drive is encrypted, or at the very least, it makes it very, very difficult for them to get access to it. Nothing is 100% foolproof, but encryption goes a long way to mitigating that risk. Then, lastly, proper disposal and sanitation processes. Just like when we want to sanitize a hard drive on a computer, we would do the same thing for a printer. We want to make sure it's wiped properly and that data is irretrievable. That way, when we dispose of that device, we know for a fact that that data is gone.

Chapter 8 Real Time Operating Systems & Surveillance Systems

Next, we have to cover RTOS, or real-time operating system. Real-time operating systems are designed to process data with minimal delay, or latency. Latency being the lag time that it takes to get a response back from something. These types of systems are more concerned with very deterministic processing of data rather than with the amount of work that can be performed. In other words, rather than being a catch-all or just a workhorse that can do everything good, this does one type of thing extremely well. They lend themselves to embedded systems, IoT devices, SCADA systems. These devices, just like any other type of operating system, even though it is a real-time operating system that's dedicated to a specific task or a subset of tasks, they still need to be updated, they still have vulnerabilities, they still need to be patched. We have to take the same due diligence with these types of systems that we do with our typical computing infrastructure. Our next area for concern is the camera systems. A lot of the security cameras that are actually used for protection are wildly open. Default username and passwords, they can get access from just the open internet. They can actually be used to monitor networks and monitor the companies that they're supposed to be protecting or guarding. A lot of these security cameras are installed with a default admin username and password, and they're never changed. A quick Google search, and I'm not recommending that you do this, but thousands of these are viewable on the internet. There's websites out there are devoted to just listing all of the cameras you can go and browse through and look at all different cameras from all over the world, where the default username and passwords are in place, and you can just view the data that they're capturing. We need to patch vulnerabilities because these things get vulnerabilities just like every other operating system or piece of computing infrastructure does, update drivers and firmware, just like any other OS or just like any other embedded system. Next, we have to understand the attack vector. Compromised cameras can be a way into a network. They can first and foremost allow us to watch what's going on, so that's not a good thing, but they're connected to a network. If we're able to actually get into that camera, elevate privileges, maintain persistence, just like with any other type of computing system, that's a way into the network. At that point, it's off to the races. We also need secure disposal policies. Encrypt communication, drives, if there are drives within those cameras, sometimes they have them, sometimes they don't, and securely wipe those devices before disposing. Next we have system on a chip, or SoC. When you SoC, it's a system on a chip, and what it means, it's an IC, or an integrated circuit, that integrates all of the components of a computer or other systems, all onto a single substrate, or a single chip. In other words, it takes an entire computer, and now it takes that entire computer, and puts it down to a chip. Some system on a chip, or SoC concerns to cover are a raspberry PI; that is an example of a system on a chip. It's an entire computing system down onto a tiny little substrate, minus the data storage. Mobile devices, phones, or wearables, watches; these are all things that are systems on a chip. These devices are becoming increasingly smaller. They used to be room sized. Then they were, suitcase sized. Now they're getting smaller and smaller for hearing aids, for vision. Next it will be down to nanotechnology or nano size, so they could inject into your bloodstream potentially, and be used to very prescriptively fight disease. Embedded devices, for hearing, for sight, for health issues; as you might imagine, there's a lot of concern here. If someone's able to compromise those devices, hackers can target those systems, compromise their data or attack the host. Let's now talk about some communication considerations. Now that 5G networks are starting to roll out globally, in the US, and across the rest of the globe, some things to worry about. Some 5G security concerns. Millions more devices will come online as 5G rolls out, and that's connected cars, healthcare. Now that we have this potential for a very high speed, very low latency network, more and more things will be tightly integrated with 5G, and we're dependent upon the network for connectivity, critical infrastructure being a big one. We talked about that before, with SCATA systems where it used to be a completely air-gapped network. That's no longer the case. Many of these systems are logically air-gapped, or, not air-gapped it all. With 5G, there are potentially more security mechanisms available; network slicing, enhanced encryption, increased visibility . But it's also more complicated to manage. The handoff between networks, as devices jump from 5G, and perhaps downgrade to 4G, or even 3G, depending upon where they are. As they traverse different parts of the landscape, they may switch networks. As that switching occurs, mechanisms that may be in place for 5G, as an example, may not have an equivalent in a 4G or a 3G network; and also something else we talked about before is supply chain attacks. As the chip manufacturers and all the sub components that make up these 5G devices are made, there is the potential for supply chain attacks, where those individual devices or components can be compromised, ultimately then putting a back door into the network or compromising it in some form or fashion. A few other terms that I want you to be familiar with are two main ones, and that's narrowband and baseband. Narrowband is designed for small amounts of data transfer, typically under 10 seconds, not milliseconds, but 10 seconds of latency. Not super speedy, but we don't really necessarily care because we're transmitting very small amounts of data. It has secure mechanisms built in, authentication and encryption, but these things are designed for very small transference of data. Then we have baseband radio, and this is dedicated processors that run real-time operating systems that we talked about before, and they control radio functions within different types of devices, not usually Wi-Fi or Bluetooth, but other radio type of connectivity. Zigbee for example at first glance, may look similar in form or fashion to Raspberry Pi or Arduino, but completely different thing we're talking about here. It's a very small device, and it's a suite of high-level communication protocols used for what's referred to as a PAN, or a personal area network. They're low power, often battery powered, low data rate, low latency, and also, close proximity wireless ad-hoc network. These things are designed to make mesh-type networks within a home, as an example. It operates in the industrial, the scientific, and medical, or ISM, radio band. There are currently over 26 billion IoT devices, and that's going to just continue to rise as we go, up into the trillions eventually. These things are becoming more and more and more ubiquitous. The average home may have 30 to 40, maybe 50 different IoT devices, and you may not even realize it. You may say to yourself, well, Zigbee, I've never even heard of it. I don't have any Zigbee devices in my house, I don't really have much to worry about. I don't care about them. Well, hold on one second there, and let's take a look at what actually makes up Zigbee products, and I'll bet that you have one or more of these things in your house. Amazon Echo as an example, Belkin or WeMo systems. I won't read through the entire list, but things like Honeywell thermostats or even Philips Hue lights. I know I have dozens of Philips Hue lights in my house. Samsung SmartThings, also their Comcast Xfinity box, and then list goes on and on. There's a very good chance you may have devices in your house that use the Zigbee protocol and you're not even aware of it. Something to keep in mind is we have some security considerations when we're talking about Zigbee security. Zigbee security does use encryption, which is good, but the keys can be extracted using publicly accessible tools, That's not so good, so you can go on the internet and search for the tools, search for the processes to do these things, It is possible. And it's also possible to jam these networks and force a repairing. If you're close enough to a device or close enough to a, let's say a person's house, you could jam their front door lock as an example. And as they get a repair, you could extract those encryption keys and potentially unlock that door. Command injection, replay attacks are possible. Also, security testing tools like SecBee, from a group called Cognosec, allows for pretty easy compromise of these devices. And again, you can easily search online for more information about these tool sets and see just how easy some of these compromises can be. When we're talking about IoT devices or embedded systems, etc, these are designed for ease of use, they are designed for low power consumption, and in some cases connectivity in hard to reach or remote locations, some of that narrow band technology that I talked about. They typically don't have large amounts of compute power, nor do they typically have the ability to manage advanced cryptographic functions like anti-tampering measures so they are potentially easy to compromise, or easier to compromise. When we have these types of devices in our house or in our businesses, all of these things come into play because they make up an attack surface, power, compute or network. If we don't have very powerful devices that are using these systems, they could be easier to compromise. Also, some of these systems, embedded systems, things that are in hard to reach places or things that are not necessarily updated very often, if at all, the inability to patch. If a vulnerability is discovered, how quickly can we patch that, if it all? Also we have authentication. If they don't have a lot of compute power or anti-tampering techniques, it may be possible to force authentication or to break authentication. Also, the range, the cost, the implied trust, all of these things come into play when we're talking about decisions around whether to bring these types of devices into our networks. Bringing these things into a corporate environment may have additional implications and you have to make sure that these things are properly vetted, properly audited, and you understand exactly how they work, what data they transmit, do they phone home, how do they phone home, what protocols do they use, what authentication methods do they use. All of these things should be vetted through you and your security teams prior to rolling them out into production. In summary we talked about embedded systems. We talked about SCADA and ICS systems. We also Talked about the Internet of Things, or IOT, along with specialized systems, voice over IP. We talked about heating, ventilation, and air conditioning, or HVAC, drones and aerial vehicles. We talked about multi-function printers and some of the security implications around those devices. We talked about real-time operating systems, or RTOS, surveillance systems and the cameras that make up those systems, system on a chip, or SoC, communication considerations, and also the constraints that we have around these systems, keeping them secure, how to patch them, how to keep them updated.

Chapter 9 Barricades, Mantraps & Alarms

In this chapter, we'll be covering Understanding the Importance of Physical Security Controls. We have physical security, talking about deterrence and controls, we'll also talk about digital and logical security such as locks, and vaults, and sensors, we'll then talk about securing infrastructure, such as protected cabling and data access, and then secure disposal of data, such as deleting and the wiping of data. Another physical control would be barricades, so barricades can prevent access by virtue of them being a physical, literally a physical, barrier. They can be temporary or they can be permanent. But even if they're permanent, they can still be fixed or movable, and they can direct the flow of traffic, or they can block traffic completely. A bollard is a giant metal pole that can rise up and go up and down to the ground. It can go down flush to allow cars to pass over, or it can rise up to provide that preventive measure. Or we have what's called a Jersey-style barrier where you'll see these a lot of times on roadways and where they want to cordon off traffic, Those things are temporary, typically, although sometimes they're put up and kept in place permanently. But these are examples of two types of barriers that can be put in place, and they can either direct the flow of traffic, or they can block traffic completely. They can be in place. They can be in raised position, and they can block traffic pretty much permanently; however, if there's an emergency, they need to get an ambulance, or they need to get some type of delivery, or something closer to the building, they can be lowered, and then, traffic or a vehicle can pass over them unrestricted. The next one is something referred to as a mantrap, and a mantrap is an access control, and it's two sets of doors. A person will enter the first set of doors, which then closes behind them, and then a guard or some automated control will allow access through a second door once

149

authentication is verified. We have one set of doors, or one door that will open, a person would walk into that enclosed area, the door would shut behind them. They either have to badge in or they have, a card reader, whether it's an RFID or NFC chip, or there may be a guard actually sitting behind a glass area, or perhaps maybe on a video camera, there's going to be some verification system that once that person is then verified, the second door will open and they can pass through. Something else that can control access is badges. Badges enable several control and visibility options, including they can provide or restrict access to individual occasions, we can badge into certain areas within the building. We can have access to one area, but not necessarily the other. They can also be revoked quickly. If someone loses access or changes roles, you don't necessarily have to go around and try to recover keys you can do that electronically via just removing access from that badge. It also provides visibility as to who is actually in the building for things like evacuations, fire drills, it makes it much easier, or at a glance, to be able to tell is everyone out of the building, who's left, because when they badge in, they're recorded, and then when they leave the building, assuming they do it correctly, they're actually listed as leaving as well. It allows for first responders to quickly identify who is in the building and who's not. Some challenges around badges, because again, nothing is foolproof, challenges are sharing and lending. It should obviously be prohibited and not allow people to share badges because again, we're now not accurately depicting who was in the building or what area they're in. Then also, if we lend badges, there's the opportunity or the chance that that could be stolen, duplicated. Tailgating should be part of corporate training, corporate policy, to not allow tailgating. In essence, someone following closely behind, you're holding the door for that person and allowing them to come in on your credentials. Everyone should have to badge in correctly, that way again, in the event of an evacuation, or fire drill, we have an accurate count of who's in the building and who's not, and then also, it just makes things more secure. If we just get in the practice of holding the door for someone, then someone who is not authorized to be there, a stranger or a bad actor could walk up, and if it's the policy to just hold the door for people, then that allows that bad actor access to the building. Next we have alarms. Alarms are common sense, but they work in tandem with other systems. They are detective, they're preventive, and they're also a deterrent. Depending upon the systems that they're working with, if, let's say for instance you have a motion detection system, as soon as motion is detected, an alarm can be sounded, so that works in tandem with that, It's a detective control type. It can be preventive in that those alarms could tie off and set off some type of workflow again where systems are locked, ports are shut down, network systems themselves could be turned off or prevented from being accessed any further, and then it could also be a deterrent in combination with signage. If people know that there's an alarm that will go off if you open this door, or if I access this system, or if I do, whatever A, B and C, if they're aware of the fact that alarms are going to be sounded, that will deter them from taking that action, typically. Combined with proper signage, it can be a very effective deterrent. If someone is truly determined to do something, this in and of itself will not fix that. A lot of people have become so conditioned to hearing alarms and hearing, , buzz and just noise in general that they don't respond to it anymore. Thieves and vandals, sometimes they understand that, if somebody hears an alarm, they're not really going to do anything, or if they do, it might take 3 to 5 minutes to realize that it's actually something significant. That gives them time to get in and get out. So don't rely solely on any one specific control type, realize that it is a combination of many things put together. Proper lighting is essential to create a safe and secure work environment. We need to make sure that we are always striving to increase safety and reduce risk by properly illuminating our workspaces. Anywhere that we have people working, we need to make sure that it's a safe environment. We also want to reduce a potential for break-ins and for vandalism and theft. It acts as a deterrent, but it won't prevent a determined thief. Preventive and detective measures are also required to give us that a triple threat. Simply having a place well-lit doesn't in and of itself prevent someone who's really determined about breaking in or doing some type of damage. As we've seen before, we have motion lights, we can have lights that are constantly illuminated, and we can have ones that are motion-controlled, If someone walks into an area, the lights come on. That in and of itself can act as a deterrent as well because they think they've been detected, for lack of a better term. Whether they're being videotaped or not, they don't know that; they see the lights come on, they think that, at least someone knows that I'm here. Working in tandem with that is signage, or proper signs. Signs are used to increase awareness and reduce risk. It's, again, a double-edged sword, It can warn of restricted areas, potential hazards, but it can also deter thieves and unauthorized individuals. We can post signs saying this area is under surveillance, this area is being monitored. We can also post signs, again, for our own employees to let them know, hey, this is a dangerous area, this is where chemicals are stored, or this is a specific area that is restricted. Make sure that we have signage in all areas anywhere where there's a potential for risk, and in other areas where we want to make sure that we let the public know, or potential vandals, thieves, let them know that the area is being monitored as well.

Chapter 10 Cameras, Video Surveillance & Guards

Video surveillance can be used to monitor access, it can be used to guard perimeters, detect motion, as well as document activity. It can also work in tandem with other mechanisms, other controls, like mantraps or remote authentication. A guard to be somewhere remote and still buzz you into an office, or a corridor, or some a place of business remotely by viewing you over a camera or some type of surveillance equipment. It can also issue alarms or alerts if unauthorized activity is detected. We can have something record and monitored 24/7, we don't have to sit there and actually watch it 24/7, but if it detects activity, it can send an alert, an email and say hey, we noticed some sounds, some movement, and you can put up zones on the different parts of the screen, and if something goes into that zone within that protected area, it can generate one type of an alert. If activities in a different zone, it can generate a different type of an alert. It can give you a little bit of granularity as to how you're alerted within the view of that camera. It also creates a record of activity for later analysis or investigation. It doesn't do much good if you have a camera sitting there, and it's not recording, or if it records over itself, every hour or every day, it should, at the very least, have a few days of runway, That you have an opportunity to go back and review, 30 days is probably optimal because that way you can go back and see some trends, or maybe pick up something that you may have missed the first time through, or if a breach or some type of unauthorized access happens, you're not necessarily going to notice that right away. If you have some time to go back and review, you can see some things that you may have inadvertently missed. In tandem with signs and other types of controls, we have guards. Guards can be a deterrent as well as a preventative control type. They can prevent access to a building or a perimeter, so they can just say you're not authorized and they do not allow access. Some guards are armed, some aren't. The guards can be on-site, and they can verify by visual sight, or they can allow access or monitor activity remotely, as we talked about before. Using video surveillance, they can look and see this is person A, this is person B, and they can tell by the visual identification via a monitor whether that person is allowed or not. So guards are a very good way to keep control and to prevent access to specific areas within your company. Next we have something referred to as a robot sentry. A robot sentry can provide 24 by 7 coverage, and these are used in such things as parking lots, garages, industrial spaces, they can be mobile, or they can be stationary. We can have guards or sentries that just simply sit at the beginning or entrance to a garage or a parking lot, and they can record the comings and goings. Or they can be mobile, and they can actually traverse through the parking lot, the garage, or some industrial space, maybe a campus. They can read license plates, they can visually inspect people walking through the premises. These things can also be remote controlled, so you can have someone at a control station who controls or maneuvers this robot through the premises. Or it can be semi-autonomous, and they just let them go, and they almost like a Roomba, where they'll just map out the location themselves, and they make their rounds appropriately. Their mere presence can provide a deterrence, and they can also deliver communications. Some robot sentries allow you to communicate through them. They have speakers. A person at a remote location can talk to someone on campus, someone walking in the parking lot, ask them who they are, or even answer questions if that person has a question as to how to get somewhere.

Generally speaking, they provide a wider range of coverage. They don't need to take breaks and all those good things other than being recharged, but they provide that presence and can also provide insight into that remote location. Another area that has the potential for deterrence is reception. A reception area, depending upon the corporate layout, the reception area can act as a deterrent and also control access, much like badges. Training is required to be aware of the social engineering tactics that some bad actors may employ. So, people who work in the reception areas should understand the different ways that bad actors may try to get past them, gather information from them. But reception areas, receptionists in general, can quickly alert security or other additional resources, as required, if something were to happen, and they also have a tribal knowledge because they work there day to day, they understand who belongs there and who is out of place. If something doesn't look they have the ability to quickly alert the proper resources, security. Next, let's talk about two-person integrity, or TPI, Two-person integrity or control. What we're talking about here is a control mechanism designed to achieve a high level of security for especially critical materials or operations. Two people must be present at all times when sensitive material is being handled, two locks on any containers containing sensitive material, and no one person may possess both keys. But these things function in military environments, nuclear facilities, even in banks. Some locks, some vaults require two keys to open the vault. It doesn't necessarily have to be something as critical as a nuclear facility, but anything that you need an added layer of security, a two-person integrity, or two-person control, makes sense. Hardware locks come in a variety of shapes and sizes and features. Some use the old-fashioned key, some are combination. Some of the newer systems are biometric devices, and that contains, a fingerprint scanner or an iris or retina scan. Something that you have, or something that you are. Those types are, I wouldn't say rare, but they're certainly not as common as the older key and combination types of locks. No matter which type you have, locks should be placed on fencing, on doors, cabinets, cages, , within your data center or within supply closets anywhere where access is restricted. And in some cases, we should even put locks on our trash cans. If we have a shredding area or something that needs to be secure, always make sure that those things are maintained because it's very easy for someone to go in a dumpster dive and pull out some sensitive information if it's not maintained properly. Next, we have biometrics, and biometrics, as you are familiar with, more than likely, is authentication based upon who you are and something that you have, whether that be a fingerprint, an iris or retina scan, a voice print. It typically ties into an access control system, which grants permissions, rights, or access once authenticated. We've seen these in a variety of shapes and sizes. That can be a single fingerprint reader. It can read a thumbprint, a fingerprint, or a whole handprint. There are also some biometrics that, like I said, can do retina scans or iris scans, they can do voice recognition. It really just depends upon the nature of the system, and it offers an additional layer of security because it's not just something that. In other words, you can't tell somebody else your pin or your password, and they go use it. It actually has something that you are, whether it be like I said, a fingerprint, voice print or iris.

Chapter 11 Cable Locks, USB Data Blockers, Safes & Fencing

When we're talking about securing physical assets, a few things to remember are cable locks. We want to make sure we secure these things to non-removable items. Common sense here, but if we don't secure our desktop or our laptop or our monitor to something that's actually non-removable, then it's very much the same as us going outside and locking our bike to an orange parking cone. You can just pick both of those things up and walk away with them. Make sure we secure these things to non-removable items. Same thing goes along with a safe. A safe is obviously there to house very sensitive or valuable information or assets, well, we want to make sure we restrict who has access to keys or the combination. It doesn't do us much good if we have a safe, we store some valuable things in that safe, and then we give everyone either the combination or a key. Doesn't do us much good, so we might as well not even have the thing. I know it sounds like common sense, but you'll be surprised. Make sure we restrict who has access to the keys or the combination. Same thing with locking cabinets. We need to make sure we restrict who has access to the keys. Typically, we're going to have things in there that we don't want everybody to have access to, so we want to limit those to a select few. That way if we only have a select few that have access to the safe, or the locking cabinet, then we only have a few people to go back to if, in fact, a breach occurs, and we can now narrow our investigation. Next, let's talk about a USB data blocker. What this does, it's a USB device that inserts between your phone or your device and a power source. It prevents hackers from accessing data on your device, otherwise known as juice jacking. We're talking about public charging stations or foreign computers, in other words, computers you don't own. If you plug into someone else's computer or you plug your phone or your device, your laptop, in this example, into a charging station, it's possible for a hacker to install some type of software, malware, viruses, that can access your device via that USB port. By having this USB blocker in place, that prevents that from happening. Malware, viruses, theft of data are prevented by using this USB data blocker device. The next one that goes hand in hand with that would be fencing. Fencing is something that we should obviously have in place around the entire perimeter of an area or a building for it to be most effective. It doesn't do us much good if we have it only around a part of our building, and they can just simply walk around the fencing and get to the rear of a building, as an example. Fencing can also have a man trap style fencing as well, so that they have to drive into an area, the fence closes behind them, they're verified, and then another gate opens up and they can pass through, so you could have that type of dual entry system in a fencing area as well. Areas inside of a data center can be fenced off as well to restrict access. It doesn't necessarily have to be just external to a company, it can also be inside of a data center. We might have an area like a caged-off area where we have some extra sensitive information, or it could be a supply area, supply closet or a loading dock. So fencing can be not necessarily for just people exterior to the company, I should say, it could also be to keep people inside the company out of specific areas as well. Fencing can be a deterrent, or it can be preventive. Depending upon the type of fence, if it's just a 2 or 3-foot tall fence or maybe a 5-foot tall fence with nothing on top, that might be a deterrent, but it's not going to prevent someone from getting over top. If you have a fence like you see here that has some type of barbed wire or even maybe worse, even some razor wire on top, well, chances are that would be preventive. I certainly wouldn't be going over a fence like that. It just depends upon the type of fence. When it comes to fire suppression, we have lots of investment. We have high dollar pieces of equipment in our data centers, in our server rooms, critical components to our business. Any data center where there is an investment in computer systems and infrastructure, we need to make sure that we have an investment in our fire suppression system as well. Fire needs three things to exist. We have heat, fuel, and oxygen. If we remove one of any of those three, then we obviously take a fire's ability to exist away, we'll put the fire out, so those things need to be there. Fire suppression systems will remove one or more of those elements, and that's what puts the fire out. If we take a look at it here, as I said, a fire suppression system removes one of the three elements that are needed for combustion. We would have canisters, we'd have sensors on the wall, and then some type of sprinkler or dispersion heads up on top. Some data centers will have sprinkler systems. Water is not the most friendly component for our data center, however, we need to have it there in the event that it's a fire raging out of control. In the event that it's a small fire or some type of preventative system, there are systems put in place, and FM-200 is one of the most widely used clean agents. It's stored actually as a liquid in canisters, there's these canisters that store typically liquid compressed with nitrogen or some type of gas, there's sensors in a control panel on the wall, and then there are sprinkler heads or dispersion heads up in the ceiling. What happens is, if heat starts to come up inside the data center, before it actually even turns into a fire, those sensors can detect, the heat itself. There's not a fire yet, it's just hot. Well, those detectors can sense that, they will then alert to the control center or the control panel on the wall. That control panel can in tandem set off an alarm, signal to our administrators but then it can also then trigger the discharge of FM-200. That quickly reaches, within 7-10 seconds, enough of a dispersion in the atmosphere or in the air to absorb all the heat. It takes the heat away out of that triangle, it takes away one of the three elements that is needed for that fire, It can absorb enough so that the fire never actually erupts. If it gets beyond that, for some reason, and it happens too quickly or the fire overruns, that's when the sprinkler heads would then kick in. There are some other agents as well, FM-200 is one. DuPont also makes FE-13, 25, and 36 that can be used to retrofit existing systems and also for fire extinguishers. It doesn't necessarily have to be a brand-new system that's put in place like an FM-200 system, but there should definitely be some type of clean agent if possible, so that you don't spray your equipment with water or some type of chemical that can be corrosive. If we can absorb the heat and take that away before the fire even has a chance to start, we're going to be in a much better position.

Chapter 12 Motion Detection / Infrared & Proximity Readers

We also have motion detection and infrared. It's a technical control that provides detective and also deterrence capabilities. It can be combined with signage, and that can be a really powerful tool against intrusion. Is going to stop everybody? No, not, but it is a deterrent. What it does is put people on notice that, hey, if you come into this area, you're under surveillance, motion detection is enabled, and what you're doing is going to be recorded. It makes people think twice about what their going to do, doesn't prevent everybody, but it's a good start. That video can be used to detect movement in real time, or it can be used for later analysis and investigation. Infrared sensors can also detect motion in complete darkness, so just because the area is not illuminated with visible light, so that allows the camera to see everything as if it were daytime. Next we have proximity readers, and proximity readers are becoming more and more commonplace. They are typically used with ID cards, and they contain either an NFC chip or some type of RFID chip. A near-field communication or some type of radio frequency ID so that you can pass your card close to the reader, but you don't actually have to be right up on it. Whether it's you show your ID card as you enter a building in the morning, maybe it lifts a gate and you can drive through into a parking lot, or perhaps maybe through some type of turnstile as you go into the building. A person doesn't need to physically touch the reader, and it works in tandem with access lists or access control systems. As you wave your badge in front of this reader, it then checks against an access list or access control list and says, yes, this person is allowed access or they're not, or it may give you certain access or access to certain areas of the building. You may be able to get into an area perfectly fine, and then you go to a more restricted area and you wave your badge again and you're not allowed access to that specific door. It gives the company itself the ability to be very granular as to what access or level of access it can grant employees as they move about and have access to certain areas within a building. We've talked about drones and UAVs before, but just to put it in the context of monitoring for physical security, a drone could provide security and monitor large areas very quickly. We have that aerial view of our footprint. Drones can also be remotely activated based on motion. We could have a drone sitting in its charging cradle or in some type of holding facility, and then as soon as motion is detected, it can release the drone, the drone goes up in the air, flies over to wherever that motion is taking place, and can record that activity or provide insight into what's going on. It can also be used to monitor sections of PDSs or protected distribution systems with a hardened cabling in a secure system that sometimes can stretch very long distances. Drones can allow the monitoring of that very efficiently. Real-time insights into security and emergency situations allowing for precise intelligence gathering, comprehensive situational awareness, depending upon the type of activity and the type of an event. Next, we have logs, and logs provide critical details required when investigating an incident, or a breach; such things as the time of incident, their credentials that were used, maybe files or servers or resources that were accessed, also any activity, and any potential methods used. If someone's trying to cover their tracks where they used some type of escalation or privileges, once they get access to a resource, they try to maintain persistence, and they try to install some type of back door, so they can get back in again, if their primary way of breaching was discovered or somehow closed off. They maintain that persistence, and they get in and try to traverse the network, perhaps hit a point where they can pivot and jump onto another network that they typically wouldn't have access to. All of those types of activities, and the resources that they use, and the methods they use, can be identified potentially, if logs are properly kept. Next to something referred to as air gaps. An air gap is a method of isolating a computer or a network from the internet or from other external networks, or other networks aside from the one you're on. It doesn't necessarily have to be just from the internet. It could be from other networks within your company. If you have a very highly secure environment that you need to make sure that there's no chance of malware or viruses being introduced, then you would set up an air-gapped network. As with anything, there is no 100% guarantee, as we've seen in the past, with things like Stuxnet and some other very highly visible and highly cited instances where malware has actually jumped into air-gapped environments, nothing is 100% certain. But anyway, it's used for critical infrastructure. SCADA systems, as an example, and I refer back to Stuxnet, where the SCADA systems were still compromised, highly secure classified networks. There are some advanced techniques, however, to jump air gap networks. That's been demonstrated. Emanations, there's actually a technology, and it's been completely demonstrated, where they can view the emanations coming off of a computer, whether it is the sound of the hard drive whirring, or even the heat being generated by the hard drive spinning up. If you're close enough to that device, you can actually pick those things up from the device and discern what's going on. You can read data from that device. It's not something the average hacker can do, but just understand that an air gap is a very good way of isolating the network, but it's not 100% foolproof. In fact, the US government, and other agencies around the world, have specific guidelines to create additional security. The US uses something referred to as TEMPEST, which protects that room, it has to be certain thickness of walls and has to have additional coding and protections, Faraday cages, and things that just prevent emanations and monitoring from nearby locations.

Emanations, FM frequencies, even some hard drives that actually a small LED light on the front that actually shows activity of that drive. You don't see that too much anymore, but it is possible, that if you have a line of sight visibility to that light going on and off as the hard drive writes, you could actually read, almost like Morse code, what's going on with that hard drive, and read data from that device. Pretty scary stuff. But, the average hacker is not going to be employing that. More than likely, you can rest assured that your home network is safe. We've discussed that an air gap is a network that is physically separated from an unsecured network, with the goal being to ensure the packets or data grams don't leave the secure network unintentionally. A few additional pieces of information, though that we should be aware of, is the fact that when we move data between networks, let's say, for instance, we have a less secure network and then a more secure network; so networks that are designed to handle different levels of classified data are referred to as the high side and the low side; low side, as you might guess, meaning the less secure; high side being very secure or more secured networks. When we're moving data from one side to the other, low side to high side is a fairly straightforward process because the high side is already able to view that information, or contain that information. However, moving data from the high side, or the confidential side, to the low side, requires more stringent processes. Those types of moves should be done manually and making sure that data does not inadvertently leak out from a secure network to an insecure network. More stringent processes, due diligence, should be put in place to ensure that that confidential data stays confidential.

Chapter 13 Demilitarized Zone & Protected Distribution System

Next, let's talk about the concept of a demilitarized zone, or DMZ. A demilitarized zone, also known as a perimeter network, or a screened subnet; so you may hear any of these terms, interchangeably. The newer, or more preferred, name, these days, is a screened subnet, but they typically consist of hosts that provide services outside of the local area network, or the internal network; such things as email servers, web servers, DNS servers. A security professional, an IT security professional or a cybersecurity professional, is not going to know every single thing about every single topic within IT security. That's like saying, oh, how to drive a car, great, go jump on that 18-wheeler. Even though they both fall under the same quote unquote category, it doesn't mean you can necessarily operate both effectively, so It's not expected that every single thing within IT security or cybersecurity, but it's a good idea to understand where all of these things fit, so you can understand architecturally how they all fit together. On our internal network, we have a number of things; Active Directory servers, DNS, servers, perhaps some type of intrusion detection or prevention systems, logging servers. We might have some database servers, and then behind that, we may have some storage; and then we also have a DMZ, or a demilitarized zone. That's going to be comprised of things we want to be public facing, but we want to secure from our internal network. We want to create a separate network, if you will, and you'll place things like your web servers, DNS, servers, your external DNS servers, mail servers, proxy servers. In this example, we have a user who wants to get to an internal network, as an example. Well the user is going to connect to the internet, ? They're going to connect via their ISP, at which point they would encounter our external firewall. Now, there, we could place an intrusion detection or prevention system, to get an idea of how many people are trying to penetrate our network, or trying to get in unauthorized. , we don't necessarily have to put it there, but we can. It can be placed in different places throughout the network. But they'll pass through the firewall. The firewall will let certain ports through, like DNS, mail, SMTP and POP and IMAP. Port 80, port 443; and then the various application servers may have individual ports that they need access to as well. We can think of this as a less secure zone than our internal network. We want to allow people to actually get into this area from the outside world, but we don't want to allow them into our internal network. We'll have another firewall between our DMZ and our internal network; and from there, again, we may choose to place an intrusion detection, or prevention, system, or we may they choose to place that on the inside; and once we get inside to our internal network, then we have Active Directory, DNS, intrusion detection and prevention systems, logging servers, database servers and storage, or our application servers. I just want you to get a general idea of how these things are laid out. The basic takeaway here, is, what is a DMZ, the demilitarized zone. Also a couple things to keep in mind; we have wireless and guest networks. We have a guest. They may have a laptop, or they may have a desktop. They may be actually someone on our network, and they want to access some external network, or an external resource. Well, how do they do that? Well, they're going to connect to a wireless access point, if they have a laptop, or some type of mobile device, or through a desktop, they may plug directly into a jack in the wall, and off they go. From there, they will access, some of the things that are laid out, a router, a switch, firewall. Well, if they're on our wireless network, they will access that wireless access point. That wireless access point will reach out to, typically, in a corporate environment, will reach out to a RADIUS server, a remote access and dial-in user service. That will authenticate that guest and give them access, or, if there's no password, it'll just let them through, but typically, in a corporate environment, you're still going to require some type of username and password. That may change every couple of weeks, every couple of months, or but they're still going to authenticate with that RADIUS server; and also a wireless LAN controller comes into play, if we have more than one wireless access point. Say we have a large corporate environment, and we have wireless access points all throughout our environment, all throughout our buildings, multiple buildings and multiple locations. Well, those wireless access controllers, or the wireless LAN controller, allow us to configure all of those wireless access points from one location. Next, we have protected distribution systems, and this deals with cabling, PDS. And a protected distribution system is a secure conduit. It can be for copper or for fiber optic cabling, and there are a couple different types we'll talk about that has monitors in place to detect any disruption to the PDS. It gives us a very secure transport mechanism. The carrier itself we can run cabling through. It's covered under the National Security Telecommunications and Information Systems Security instruction, or the NSTISSI 7003, if you want to look that up. And it was enacted December of 1996 by the Committee on National Security Systems. These types of things are in place when we're dealing with typically data carrying national security type information. There are two main classifications, and that is hardened distribution systems and then simple distribution systems. We'll cover each here in a little more detail. These are very secure access points. The cabling, it runs along this conduit, this trough that you see, but every single area, or every single point of that conduit or that carrier is sealed off. It's got epoxy, it's got very stringent guidelines as to how it's constructed. And then anywhere where there is an actual access point, it's locked, and so only specific people have access to those tie-ins, or to those areas where they can access certain sections of the cabling. First off was a hardened distribution system, or a hardened carrier, and that conduit is electrical metal tubing, ferrous conduit, or pipe. If it's going to be underground, it needs to be buried and encased in concrete. Or if it's above ground, it needs to be permanently sealed, welds, epoxy, or some other sealant. Very high secure transport mechanism. These carriers are meant to not be disturbed. There was also some guidelines that say they have to be visually inspected or visually monitored at all times if they're not buried underground. Next would be an alarmed carrier. If we're not going to have someone actually visually looking at these things constantly, then the alarm carrier gives us the ability to have fibers that actually run within the conduit that are used for monitoring acoustic vibrations. That's associated with attempted access. If someone's trying to disrupt or access any of these carriers, that fiber will detect that and then sound an alarm. That reduces the need for visual inspection and monitoring. It ties into, like I said, an automated system. An example here is that this would detect any type of vibration, it triggers an alarm, and then this device would turn around and set off some type of workflow, alerts, alarms, and send guards to the area, and so on. It can detect where along the conduit that actual disruption is occurring. Then, we have a continuously view carrier, that's another category, and that conduit is continuously viewed, as the name implies, monitored 24x7x365. Guards and security personnel will investigate any and all attempts to disturb the PDS, typically within 15 minutes. That's according to the guidelines that we talked about earlier. Those things are constantly monitored. There's someone that keeps these things up to date and views 24x7x365. National security type information. Any disruption, guards are immediately alerted, and within 15 minutes they should be on-site responding to that area of disturbance. Next, we have a simple distribution. In a simple distribution system, cables can be installed in any type of carrier, it can be made of any type of material. However, the joints and access points are monitored by personnel, and the people that actually monitor that carrier should be cleared to the highest level of data handled by that PDS. In other words, if that specific section of cabling or that carrier is carrying secret data versus top secret, or whatever the case might be, the people that actually monitor that should have that same level of clearance. In other words, someone who has secret should not be monitoring a top secret, and vice versa. If you have top secret, obviously you can monitor anything from that point down, but it should be at the highest level of data being carried through that carrier, or through those cabling. Periodic inspections are required. It needs to be continuously verified that these systems are, in fact, secure. Another environmental control that I want to call your attention to is the concept of hot and cold aisles. Data centers can contain hundreds, thousands, tens of thousands of servers, networking equipment, storage arrays, and so on. As you can imagine, all of those devices generate a lot of heat. Massive amounts of heat are generate from these devices. Even if you have in your house maybe 1 or 2 computers, maybe a server, an Xbox, PS3 or PS4, if you sit behind those things and they've been on for a while, you can understand they generate a lot of heat. Take that same amount, times that by 100 or 1000, it gets very, very warm in a data center, especially a large data center, that's why HVAC is Important. But also in tandem with that is the concept of a hot and cold aisle. So hot and cold aisles help reduce heating and cooling because, again, our compute network and storage runs more efficiently when it's cooled properly. HVAC is also going to run more efficiently when it's designed properly. Instead of simply placing equipment in a data center of wherever we can, wherever it fits, it's much more to our benefit to set it up in such a fashion that we are taking advantage of hot and cold aisles and we're maximizing our HVAC. The basic concept is to place the front of the systems on either side facing each other so that cool air can be drawn on that aisle, or infused into that aisle, drawn in from those sides, and then the opposing aisles would go back to back so that the heat blows out the back of those systems. Those will then be the hot aisles, and the hot aisles is where we'll have our HVAC pull that heat out and then either recycle it or however that HVAC system is set up. Typically, we're going to recycle that air, it's filtered. It maintains a very clean atmosphere. If we look at it a little bit more in depth, we also have the concept of hot and cold containment aisles. In a hot air containment aisle, we have an enclosed area with doors that lead in, and in the enclosed area will be the hot aisle, so we're containing the heat. That way, we can suck it out of that area and run it through our filtration system again. In the opposing aisles, which are open, would be our cold aisles. The reverse of that would be a cold air containment aisle. In a cold air containment, we actually have our sliding doors, and we keep that area of the data center, or those aisles rather, cold. By containing it, in other words, having those doors slide across, we can contain, whether it's hot or cold, we can contain that area much more efficiently. We're ensuring that our hot areas are, where our HVAC vents are, we're going to pull that hot air out, and then we're going to place cold air in, so it gets filtered through.

Chapter 14 Shredding, Pulping & Pulverizing

Let's go ahead and start off and talk about the non-digital data destruction, or things that are not necessarily data on magnetic media, flash drives, In other words, paper documents. Really four things we can do here. We can talk about burning, and we'll cover each of these in more detail in just a second, but first off, we have burning, which is, as the name implies, we would incinerate that data, that paper data, in some form or fashion. Next we have shredding, and there are various types of shredders, we'll cover those more detail in just a moment. Then we have something referred to as pulping and then pulverizing. Then when it comes to digital data destruction, we have also something referred to as pulverizing. We then have degaussing, degaussing, depending upon, where you read or who you hear pronounce it. Then we have purging, and then wiping. Let's cover each of these error more detail. When we talk about burning, documents are incinerated, it's put into a fire, whether it is simply thrown into someone's fireplace, or there are actual commercial incineration facilities, where you can put bulk documents in and burn them down to unrecoverable status. It can also be combined with other methods to increase security, such as shredding, pulping, or pulverizing, meaning we could take one of those methods first, shred it, pulp it, or pulverize that paper data, and then incinerate at the end, We would cut it up into small pieces, whether the shredding is long strip or across cut, as an example, and then when that's done, we would then incinerate those documents, At that point, there's pretty much zero chance that data is going to be recovered. Then next, we have shredding. With shredding, documents are cut into small pieces. We have long-cut shredders, which are most typically found in like residence and small office home office environments; however, those long-cut shredded documents are not considered secure because if you take enough time and you have enough people working on it or if you just painstakingly, attention to detail, you can take each of those strips, those long strips, and find out the matching pieces and put that data back together, put those documents back together, much like you would put a jigsaw puzzle back together. It's time consuming, but it's possible. They're not considered secure. Cross-cut, on the other hand, where custard into very small pieces, much like confetti, is more secure, but it's also slower and typically more expensive. If you have a bulk documents, you typically would want to take these things to some type of shredding facility that has very large-scale shredding equipment that can do these things en masse. Then we have something referred to as pulping. Pulping is a process, where those documents are put into a vat, or a bin of some sort, and then a solution is poured in, and those documents are soaked in that solution until it is reduced to what's referred to as a slurry. It's just a mush. That data on those paper documents are then at that point, unrecoverable. Pulp can be reused, or recycled. It can actually be used to make new paper. It can be expensive. It's also time consuming, and one of the challenges can be, if you have a large number of documents, you're destroying documents at a large scale, that can be also difficult to transport because, because you won't normally have those facilities on site, so you have to transfer all of those documents to that facility. Next, we have something referred to as pulverizing. Now pulverizing can be used for paper documents. It can also be used for digital media. If we're talking about storage media, as an example, the media is fed into a pulverizing machine, which literally crushes those drives, whether it's a flash drive, a magnetic disk, a spinning hard disk. It will crush that material, or those drives, into small pieces. Hydraulic or pneumatic action, much like a very heavy duty pneumatically fed shredder. It is used to reduce that media to loose fibers, if we're talking about paper, or to shards, if we're talking about storage media, it just breaks it up into small pieces. The data is not recoverable at that point.

Chapter 15 Deguassing, Purging & Wiping

Next, we have something referred to as degaussing or degaussing. There are two types here. We have either AC or DC erasure techniques, and with degaussing, if you're using AC, it applies an alternating field over time, that renders that data unrecoverable, so it takes the magnetic field on that magnetic disk and reverses it, or in some manner, obliterates it, makes it very random That the data cannot be recovered off of that drive. DC, on the other hand, will saturate the media with a unidirectional field. In either case, it's going to make that data unrecoverable. Something else to keep in mind with this process, however, is that hard drives are typically unusable after degaussing. And that is because it erases the low-level formatting that is usually done at the factory at the time of manufacture. That low-level formatting actually delineates where the tracks and sectors are on that hard drive, and the degaussing will actually remove that information from the disk. Even though the disk is wiped, there is no delineation anymore of where the tracks and sectors are, much like if you have fence posts or fence lines in a field. If there are no fences, we have no idea where to put one piece of information versus the other. With that being gone, the rewrite heads have no idea of to actually where to start and stop on that disk. It renders that disk unusable, unless, unless you take it back to the manufacturer to be low-level formatted, or you have some type of tool provided by the vendor to low-level format that disk, which is 9 times out of 10, not done. It's just cheaper just to throw the drive away. The point being after you degauss something, don't think you're just going to pull that drive back out of the degaussing machine and put it back into your computer and use it. It's a very good chance that

that drive is going to be unusable. Next up, let's talk about something referred to as purging. Purging, also known as sanitizing, removes the data, makes it unrecoverable, and also removes something referred to as data remanence. So once a disk is purged or sanitized, data cannot be reconstructed by any known methods. That's the takeaway from that process. It's typically considered a step beyond wiping of data, and it's performed in situations where highly sensitive data exists, and again, the removal of that data remanence, In other words, ghost images or little snippets of data that can be left behind that could potentially be reconstructed to reconstitute that data, It removes any of that data remanence. Next, we have wiping. Wiping is a term you may be familiar with, wiping versus deleting. When you wipe data, wiping overwrites the data x number of times, and x is a configurable number, it's a variable, but it can overwrite that data x number of times to ensure that it's unrecoverable. The number of passes, can be configured, can go from 1 up to 35 or more. In modern times with modern disks, modern hard disks, spinning drives, a single pass, a single overwrite of that data is considered unrecoverable. That is configurable, there are different methods. With SSD or flash drives, disk sanitization, what we do here is reset the NAND, the actual flash chips on the drive itself and mark all those blocks as empty. Each SSD manufacturer typically will have their own secure erase, and that's a technology run method, to have their own version or their own secure erase tool that's specific for that particular flash drive. It's effective at rendering that data unrecoverable so if that security's algorithm and the implementation of it is actually done properly. Just to dig in for a moment, some data wiping methods, there are three that we can talk about here. One is DoD 5220.22-M standard, and that's the Department of Defense standard for a three-pass overwrite. That is considered secure and makes that data unrecoverable, pass 1 writes a 0 and verifies the write, pass 2 writes a 1 and verifies the write, and then pass 3 writes a random character and then verifies the write. We're talking about wiping an entire disk and making that disk now available or properly sanitized so it can be reused or repurposed in some fashion. Next is the RCMP CSEC ITSG-06, so that's the Communication Security Establishment of Canada. The RCMP, which has a great set of tools, they're very highly regarded in the forensics and cyber-investigative space, they have a three pass as well. Pass 1 writes a 1 or a 0, pass 2 writes a complement of the previously written character. In other words, it will write a 1 if pass 1 was a 0. so pass 2 would be a 1 if pass 1 was 0 or vice versa. Then pass 3 writes a random character and verifies that write. It makes sure that that data is obliterated; it cannot be recovered. And then we have secure erase, which I mentioned, that's a single pass, and it writes a binary 1 or 0. It's going to overwrite that data. It's very fast, and it's only available, for whole disk sanitization. The other two methods, they can wipe individual files, but typically, when we're talking about making a disk available for reuse or properly disposing of assets, we're talking about wiping the entire disk, whole disk sanitization. In summary, we talked about physical security, the different types of deterrents and the different types of controls that can make that security happen. We talked about digital and logical security, the different types of locks, and vaults, and sensors. Then we talked about securing infrastructure with our PDS, or protected cabling, and then the various types of data access restriction. Then we wrapped up with a secure disposal of data, both physical data, paper data and also digital data, deleting and wiping and securely getting rid of information we no longer need.

Chapter 16 Cryptographic Terminology and History

In the following chapters, we'll be covering Understanding the Basics of Cryptographic Concepts. We'll be talking about digital signatures and the concept of cipher suites, such things as salting and hashing. We'll also go over at a high level quantum communications and quantum computing. We'll also talk about blockchain, steganography, and some common use cases, as well as limitations. Why should I really care? What does this mean for me? Well, first off, encryption is everywhere, and it can work either for us or against us, so it's imperative that we understand how it works, what's appropriate to use, and when and where, and also to make sure we understand what's not appropriate. Not understanding what's appropriate could also be costly, not just in terms of financially to the company, but to brand, reputation, customer confidence, investor confidence, your job, There's a lot of things at stake here if we don't do things properly. Even if you're not tasked directly with some of the things covered in this chapter, security is everyone's responsibility, It's very important that each and every one of us understand at a fairly deep level what these things mean, what's appropriate and not appropriate, when we should be using a specific technology or a specific algorithm and when we should not. Let's start off and cover some cryptographic terminology. Starting off, cryptography, what is that? Well, that is the practice and the study of hiding information. Cryptography is actually a pretty old science, if you will, part art, part science. It dates back 4000 years. Next, we have cryptanalysis, and that is discovering some weakness or an insecurity in cryptography, so our cryptographic scheme. We're looking for some hole or vulnerability, and so we have two competing technologies, or competing sciences, here.

We have one who is the cryptographer, and that person is trying to hide information, and then the person who's tasked with cryptanalysis, they're actually trying to discover some weakness in that cryptographic scheme. Next, we have encryption, and that is the method of transforming data, typically which is plain text, into an unreadable format. Then we have plain text, which is, again, the readable format of data before being encrypted. These are just some words that you should be familiar with when we're having our discussion on cryptography. Next we have ciphertext, and that is the scrambled "format of data" after it's encrypted. so we have the plain text, which is the human readable form. We're going to apply some cryptographic algorithm, or cipher, turning into ciphertext, and that's scrambled data then, again, is human unreadable. We'll need to have some method of decrypting that, and that's where you come in with decryption. that's the method of turning that ciphertext that we just talked about back into plain text, back into that human readable form. Next is the encryption algorithm, and that is a set of rules or procedures that's going to define how we actually encrypt and decrypt the data, and that's known as the encryption cipher. We'll talk about a few different ways of doing that, whether it's asymmetric, symmetric, block versus stream. We'll cover those in more detail in just a few moments. Next, the concept of a key, and that's a value used in the encryption process to encrypt and also to decrypt data, otherwise known as a cryptovariable. Just a brief bit of cryptography history. Cryptography is actually over 4000 years old, so it predates, a lot of languages itself. It predates computers, obviously, electronics or any technology. I don't think there was anybody walk around with iPhones or even Walkmans back 4000 years ago. Cryptography is a very old way of hiding information from one another. Then the earlier cryptographers reliable

177

methods simply to scramble text, otherwise known as a cipher, and they use something called a substitution cipher or a transposition cipher, It didn't advanced to the point where we have mathematical algorithms like we do now in elliptic curve and quantum cryptography, which we'll talk about later in this chapter. But back in those days, in the early days, it was simply just substituting like an A for a B, moving things left to right a certain number of characters. If you look at a substitution cipher as an example, that's changing one character for another. now Caesar, otherwise known as a Caesar cipher or a shift cipher, Julius Caesar was one of the first cryptographers or one of the first people that actually, I should say, implemented cryptography, and that was the process of shifting all the letters a certain number of spaces in the alphabet, alright. As you see here, the alphabet is shifted by three spaces, It would be X, B equals y, C equals Z, and so on We're shifting everything three spaces. Next is something referred to as ROT-13, or Rotation-13, and that is a substitution cipher as well that's going to rotate letters 13 spaces. Not extremely sophisticated. If we know the encryption algorithm, in this case, ROT-13, it's very easy to go backwards. Once we have the scrambled text, we can decipher that relatively easily. Next we have something referred to as a Vigenère table, and this is a multi-alphabet substitution cipher - a poly-alphabetic substitution cipher. It consists of your message and a keyword that only you and the other person will know. You need to share that keyword, but your keyword will go on the left, your message will go on the top, and to make things more difficult to guess, you should take the spaces out of your message. We're going to have our message, and then we're going to have our keyword, and that keyword will repeat over and over again until it fills up the length of our message. If the other person doesn't know that keyword, it's going to be very difficult for them to decipher that; however, as I said with a computer, they could brute force that because in reality it's 26 to the n-1, the n being the length of the keyword, That's how many variations there would have to be in a brute force attack before you would exhaust all possibilities. But with a very powerful computer, that is very doable. A Vigenère cipher is really not considered a secure algorithm or a secure way of communicating outside of just maybe friends passing messages, but if you want to do anything that has a high degree of security, this would not be the method that I would choose.

Chapter 17 Digital Signatures, Key Stretching & Hashing

Digital signature is an asymmetric encryption algorithm. It uses that two-key system. The two keys are mathematically linked, public-key/private-key. When we're talking about a digital signature, let's use the concept of sending or signing an email. We have Bob and Alice - old friends. She wants to send an email to Bob. Bob already has Alice's public key on his key ring. Most email programs can already accomplish this and manage these keys automatically. Alice is going to go ahead and send her email. She'll use a hashing algorithm, whether it's SHA-1, SHA-2, MD5, whatever the case might be, there's some hashing algorithm in place. She will hash that email, she'll get a hashing value. She will then encrypt that hashing value with her private key. that equals a signed document, so now that document has her digital signature attached to it, which again confirms her identity, provides non-repudiation. So going forward, Alice will now send that email to Bob, and as we mentioned, Bob will have Alice's public key already on his system. When she sends that message, she sends that signed message to him, he will use her public key to unencrypt, pull out that hashing value, hash the email, make sure the hashing values match so we can be sure that the email has not been tampered with. We can also ensure that it was sent from Alice. That offers non-repudiation, and so Bob can rest assured that that email did in fact come from Alice. Next we have a concept of key stretching, and there are two things here that we should understand. One is PBKDF2, and that stands for Password-Based Key Derivation Function 2. It's up to you if you'd rather remember that or just say PBKDF2. If you want to sound really smart, use the acronym, because nobody knows what it means, but be prepared to answer if they do ask you. nothing worse than using an acronym trying to sound smart, and then someone says, what's that mean? Password-Based Key Derivation Function 2, it's part of RSA, It's a pseudorandom function applied to a password or a passphrase. That's the thing we have to understand. The whole concept of key stretching is the fact that perhaps our key is not as strong as it could be. Well, we can strengthen that by, in effect, stretching that key, whether it be a hash, a cipher, or an HMAC. We can also have something called a password salt, or a salt rather, to the password. When we salt something, we're adding some additional randomization to that password or to that passphrase. By doing that, it exponentially increases how much more difficult that is to break, brute force, rainbow tables because it's not the same thing over and over and over again. Every time it gets used, that salt changes it just a bit, so it's almost like the one-time pads, where if you rip the page off, it's not completely different. By adding a salt, salting that password, whether it's whatever mechanism that might be, that added randomness makes it more difficult. The process is also repeated many times. As we do that, let's say we go through all this process, we do a hash, we add a salt or an HMAC, that's one pass. We can do it again and again, and each time we do that, it makes it that much more difficult to try to reverse engineer that. It just makes it much more challenging, given today's resources, for someone to hack, or crack rather, that password or that hash. If in fact they do, the next time they try to do it again, it's not the same anymore. The salt has been added, so it changes it up. Ultimately, it creates a derived key. That derived key, again, is random to a certain degree, and that can be used for future communications or for subsequent communications. That pseudorandom process makes it much more difficult. Even if the person might know the passphrase or they may know a piece of the equation that would typically be passed between sender and recipient, that salting, that randomization, and the subsequent derived key makes it a different encrypted component and makes it that much more difficult for them to decrypt. Well bcrypt is another example. Bcrypt is actually something that was developed in 1999, and it was developed based upon the Blowfish algorithm. And what it does is provide key derivation functions, gives us that added randomness used for passwords. It allows us to strengthen the key, even though that key may not be strong in and of itself. It gives us some additional characteristics we can add to that key. It adds additional functions, such as salting. When we salt a password, we strengthen it by adding randomization. Just like you add salt to food to make it better, when we salt a password, we're really making it better or making it stronger, so that salt function adds that randomness. Each time it goes through, the salting is different, which makes the encryption different, so it makes it much harder to crack, and as you see, it helps to guard against rainbow table attacks. Next, let's talk about hashing. Hashing is a mathematical algorithm that's applied to a file before and after transmission. If anything within that file changes, the hash will be completely different. We have a couple options. We could use MD5, SHA1, or SHA2, and that's your choice, depending upon which algorithm you want to use; they will each produce a different result. In this example, have a SHA1 algorithm that I will apply to the sentence! I'll run a SHA1 algorithm against that, and you'll see the resultant answer. If I change one letter in this example, I'll take the exclamation point off the end of that file and run that SHA1 hash again, you'll see the answer is completely different. By simply changing one letter in that sentence, it gives us a completely different hashing answer. In the real world, if we hashed an entire file or an entire disk, if anything has changed on that disk or in that file, depending on the example, it will result with a different hash file. Whether we're trying to send something to someone, we could take a hash first and then let them hash again when they get on the other side and see if the numbers match. If they match, we know nothing's changed; it hasn't been manipulated. Or from a forensics point of view, as an example, we could dig a hash of an entire hard drive. Then anytime you want to prove the veracity of that image, we can just run a hash against that again, and as long as those numbers match, we know that nothing has changed on that hard disk.

Chapter 18 Quantum Communications & Elliptic Curve Cryptography

An out-of-band key exchange is not sent over the network. That needs to be delivered via traditional means or manually, either in person, over the telephone, via courier. I have to get that secret key to the recipient, not sending it over the network, so that takes away the ability for it to be compromised, at least electronically, if someone is eavesdropping. An in-band key exchange, by comparison, is actually done over the network as the communication session is established. It's done real time as we're setting up communication with the other person. It's typically discarded once the session is over, it's usually used for that one-time communication, but just understand the difference between in-band and out-of-band. Out-of-band is more cumbersome, but it's also a little more secure for certain types of communication because there's no chance of someone, if they happen to be sniffing the wire at that point in time, they're not going to be able to pull that information off the wire potentially. With some of our other examples, if I want to call someone up and say, hey, my secret password is XYZ, now we both know that password, we can communicate using that password that only I and the recipient know. There's always that big what-if. If someone happens to be tapping the phone or they read the mail or there's always ways that things can be sniffed, but we're talking about a real-time pulling-off-the-wire, if you will, of those secret keys while that communication session is being established, That's just the main differentiation between these two pieces. Next we have Elliptic Curve Cryptography, and this is otherwise known as ECC. This is an asymmetric encryption that uses the algebraic structure of elliptic curves rather than the mathematical backend to generate these random keys and generate these secret keys between two systems. By using the elliptical curves and using the points on those curves, we can generate strong encryption keys, but yet use a smaller key size. You don't have to rely on all the computational resources to generate those very strong keys. The asymmetric encryption normally requires a very large amount of resources. Some of these keys are extremely big, and when we're using this to in fact encrypt this data, obviously it takes a lot of backend processing power. If we can use smaller keys and still achieve the same amount of security, well, then that's a good thing. You don't really have to understand the depths of how this works for the exam, just understand that Elliptic Curve Cryptography uses that algebraic structure, and it achieves the same level of security using smaller keys or smaller key size than traditional encryption algorithms. It gives us that same level of security using less processing power. If you contrast that with perfect forward secrecy, session keys that are derived from a set of long-term keys, yet discrete in nature. What do I mean by that? Well, if one of the long-term keys is compromised, it doesn't compromise that session key or the data that it protects. That's why I said, these keys, these session keys, are derived from the long-term keys, yet they're discrete, they're not mathematically linked. If the long term-key gets compromised, it does not compromise that session key. There are some additional rules that apply to this. Keys used to protect data aren't used to derive any additional keys. That makes sure that each session key and each communication that is protected by that is discrete in that fact. The keys used to protect are not used to derive any additional keys. And then if the keys used to protect the data currently were derived from some additional or some other keying material, then that material must not be used to derive any additional keys. The takeaway here is we want to make sure that each communication session uses its own discrete set of keys that are not linked to any other keys. That way, if one session gets compromised, the long-term key gets compromised, it does not actually compromise any individual communication session. Next let's talk about quantum communications. This is obviously a very deep field, a very emerging field, and not something that's actually in common practice widespread yet, but it's definitely coming and definitely something that we want to be familiar with. Quantum communications is predicated on the fact or the principles of quantum mechanics and the various properties contained therein. One thing we should be aware of is the concept of quantum entanglement. Quantum entanglement states that two particles can be joined, or entangled, regardless of the space that separates them. It could be across the room, it could be across the country, or theoretically across the universe. Quantum entanglement of two particles separated in space. Also, communications will take place between these two parties using something called quantum key distribution, and we'll talk more about that in just a moment. That's the basics, two of the principles that make up quantum communications. That creates, that quantum key distribution, creates an intrinsically secure and totally random keying material based upon quantum mechanics. Because, as we'll talk about it later, when we use random number generators, or pseudorandom number generators, those things can ultimately be predicted, given enough time and computing power, whereas using quantum key distribution and the properties of quantum mechanics, it's completely random, there is no way to predict that. By using that completely random keying material, we start off from a very secure base, and then everything that's built upon that becomes intrinsically more secure. As an example, here we have Bob and Alice. As we talked about before, they are old friends since the start of the internet, back in the late '60s, they've been good friends. Well, Bob and Alice, they want to communicate, so they have their laptops and they want to communicate with each other using quantum communications, so they want establish a quantum communication channel. And without getting too, too deep into the process behind the scenes, there's something referred to as that quantum entanglement that I mentioned. So Bob will generate two photons using specialized equipment, those photons are entangled, one photon will be sent to Alice, and she will receive it. But now remember, those photons are entangled, so that starts off the key distribution and they're going to agree on how to communicate. Well if Eve, the hacker, Eve, is now eavesdropping. Eve is actually listening in on the communication, or trying to, well as soon as he does that, the mere act of observing that particle, which is an element of quantum mechanics, the mere act of observing something changes it's state. It's beyond the scope to really dig into that too deeply here, but just understand that the act of even looking at, or eavesdropping on that communication, changes the state of that particle. Since these particles are entangled, they're conjoined, what happens on the side that Alice has instantly also changes the particle on Bob's side. He can tell in an instant that that communication has been intercepted or is being listened in on. The act of observing or eavesdropping on those quantum particles changes its properties, instantly changing the associated entangled particle as well. That lets Bob know, hey, someone's listening in, they drop that communication, they send new particles, and they agree again. If it continues to be eavesdropped on, they know that they're not secure and they can either not communicate, or they can choose obviously to communicate in an unsecure fashion or insecure fashion, but at this point they know that someone is listening or eavesdropping on that communication.

Chapter 19 Quantum Computing, Cipher Modes & XOR Function

We're talking about quantum computing, again, an emerging field of computing, It's not widely spread yet, but it is coming, It's something we have to be prepared for. It's more powerful at certain tasks than classical computing, and it uses something called Qbits instead of regular bits, a 0 or a 1 in traditional or classical computing. Qbits are something a little bit different. Qbits can exist in one of three states, either on, or off, or both on and off at the same time, like the old Schrodinger's cat, was it alive or dead, or is it alive and dead at the same time, if you're familiar with quantum mechanics or quantum physics in any form or fashion. Beyond the scope of this book to dig into it, but just understand that quantum computing is a specific type of computing process or power that will, at some point in time, when it becomes mainstream, will in effect be able to break traditional cryptography, along with other things. It's very, very good at doing certain types of tasks because it can do almost all tasks that assigned to it simultaneously, whereas normal computers can do things and maybe parallel or serial, but they don't do every single thing at once. Even though there's some parralization. With quantum computing, certain tasks can be done simultaneously. It can break certain things that take quite a long time, if not indefinitely with today's traditional or classical computing. Quantum computing will be able to bypass that. That brings us to post quantum. We haven't even gotten to quantum yet, what are we talking about post quantum? Well, cryptographic algorithms that can withstand quantum computing attacks, so financial transactions, federal and military data, medical devices, autonomous vehicles, the list goes on and on. These things need to be secured against quantum computing. If a hacker or a bad actor is able to get their hands on a quantum computer and use it for bad purposes, they could, in effect, have a massive impact on these transactions, on these industries, along with everything else. Several years ago, NIST called for a post quantum proposal. They put the call to action out there, and they're looking for people to submit their ideas and their plans for post quantum cryptography, or cryptographic algorithms that can withstand quantum attacks. They're currently in round three of submissions, and the draft is expected in 2022-2024, somewhere in that timeframe. It's expected to have quantum-proof cryptography or some algorithms that are quantum proof, somewhere in that 2022-2024 timeframe. Next we have a concept of ephemeral key, and the very term ephemeral means temporary. An ephemeral key is a temporary key that's used only once. It can be reused during a single communication session, but once that communication session is over, the key is gone. it can also be used to derive an additional key that is used for subsequent communications. I want to contrast this with forward secrecy that we're going to talk about in just a moment. Ephemeral keys are used only one time or throughout a single communication session, however, they can be used to derive additional keys for subsequent communication. Two cipher modes that I want to touch on, first, is counter mode, or CTR, and that's a random 64-bit block that's used as the first initialization vector. these are algorithms, or methods, that are used to encrypt data. It increments a specified number for each subsequent block of plain text. That way, each block is slightly different, It gives them randomization to that encryption cipher. Second is the Galois counter mode, or GCM, and this is used with symmetric key block ciphers, it's very efficient, low latency, and it also adds data integrity. So rather than dig deeply into what these things do and how they operate, at this point, I just want you to understand what they are and the high level basics of how they function. Next we have the XOR function. XOR, or eXclusive OR, is a method to obfuscate data. What we do is we compare two binary strings of data to produce an output. Two matching bits produces a "false," or an output of 0. Two dissimilar bits produces a "true," or an output of 1. As we see here, we have two strings of data. One is the original data, which is binary. The second line here is our cipher, and in this case, it's just 1100 repeated for the length of the original data or the original text. They are dissimilar, They will produce a true output, or an output of 1. Conversely, on the very end, we have an example of 2 similar bits, two 0s, or it could also be two 1's. As long as those 2 digits match, that's going to be an output of 0, or false. The resulting output with MBR encrypted text. Without knowing what that cipher is, it could be very difficult, if not impossible, to reverse that and get the original text. As long as we have that cipher, though, we can match things up and then very quickly revert back from our encrypted text back to the original data. Let's now talk about cryptographic methods and design, and there's a few things we have to cover. First is ECB or Electronic Code Book, next will be CBC or Cipher Block Chaining Mode, and then we have OFB or Output Feedback Mode, and then CFB or Cipher Feedback Mode. Let's look at each of these individually. In Electronic Code Book, or ECB, we see here that plain text is discreet blocks that are encrypted separately, so we see here each of these individual blocks produces the same ciphertext each time. When we're doing this key, the same key is applied against the plain text. If we have the same, let's say the same sentence, and we encrypt that over and over and over again, or the same word as an example, and we encrypt that over and over and over again, that same word will produce the same ciphertext each time. ECB should only be used for small amounts of data, when we're transmitting small amounts, because we have less chance to observe a pattern. If we're going to transmit large amounts of data with ECB, it becomes very easy to distinguish that pattern over and over and over again, and out of all of the encryption methods that we're covering here, it's the easiest to crack, so, again, only use for small amounts of data. Next would be Cipher Block Chaining Mode, or CBC. The introduction of something called an initialization vector. CBC is similar to Electronic Code Book, except that CBC inserts or something called XOR, it XORs some of the ciphertext created from the previous block. In other words, the IV or initialization vector is introduced in the very first block, so it's the seed, if you will. That's introduced along with the plain text, and a key creates your ciphertext. That ciphertext is then used, or part of that ciphertext is then inserted into the stream. That insertion is referred to as an XOR process. That's inserted into the next block. Blocks are chained together, hence the term Cipher Block Chaining Mode. Each subsequent block relies on some of the encryption or some of the ciphertext from the previous block to encrypt that block and then subsequent blocks, so on and so on and so on. The XOR process is simply inserting some of the previous ciphertext from the previous block into the next block. Then next, we have Output Feedback Motor, OFB, and again, OFB similar, looks similar, but there's some nuances here. Output Feedback Mode makes a block cipher into a stream cipher. The entire output of the previous block is used as the input for the next block's encryption. As we see as we go through here, the first block is encrypted, that entirety of that block is then introduced or used to encrypt the second block. Now the way this works, and a key differentiation between this method and the next method I'll talk about in just a moment, is the fact that transmission errors do not propagate throughout that encryption process. That's the key takeaway there, Output Feedback Mode versus Cipher Feedback Mode, or CFB. Cipher Feedback Mode is similar to OFB, and that can also be implemented as a stream cipher. However, ciphertext is streamed together, and so that allows that error or corruption to propagate through the encryption process. As you go through the four methods we just talked about, just understand where the plain text starts off, where the initialization vector starts off, where that XOR process takes place, and then also the differentiation between output feedback and cipher feedback. One does not propagate errors and one does. That's the takeaways as far as that is concerned.

Chapter 20 Encryptions & Blockchains

Blockchain is an immutable, decentralized digital ledger that is distributed among a network of many computers, a peer-to-peer network. Once a transaction is recorded in this ledger, it can't be altered or removed, or at least, not very easily. It's extremely tamper resistant. This provides trust, transparency, and near real-time processing of transactions. A block is a batch of transactions with a cryptographic hash of the prior block, a time stamp, and some other information. That digital hash, as well learn just a second, links these blocks together or makes a blockchain. Editing or altering a block would change all of the blocks that follow it, and I'll talk about that more in just a moment. You can think of it as a digital ledger, much like a checkbook would be in a checking account. It is a ledger of all transactions, everything that gets done gets entered line by line into that ledger. Blockchain was actually initially conceived way back in 1991 as a timestamp for digital transactions; however, it didn't really gain any recognition or acceptance until it was adopted in 2009 by Satoshi Nakamoto, and we don't really know if he's a real person, if it's a pseudonym, or a group of people, no one seems to know for sure. But it was developed by Satoshi Nakamoto for use with Bitcoin. Everyone is familiar with Bitcoin, cryptocurrency, and sometimes folks will commingle those terms and think that blockchain is Bitcoin or cryptocurrency. They are two distinct things. Bitcoin and cryptocurrency utilize the underlying technology of blockchain, but they're not exactly the same thing. Blockchain can exist outside of cryptocurrency. Each block contains a number of different things. It contains data, it contains a hash of that data, and then also a hash of the previous block. The data that that actual block contains will vary depending upon the type of blockchain that it is. If it's Bitcoin or cryptocurrency, it'll have a certain set of data. If it's used for supply chain, or medical devices, or you name the industry, there's different types of blockchains for different types of things, each chain will contain different types of data, it's not always the same; however, the hash and the hash of the previous block, that will remain regardless of the type of blockchain that we're talking about. We have our blockchain, and you can see, we have some data on that block, we have a hash of that block, and then the hash of the previous block. Now, since this is the very first block, there is no hash of the previous block, that's referred to as a Genesis block. Next, you can see the next block in that chain has a hash of the previous block. That creates that linkage between the two blocks. It's going to have its own data, and then a hash of that data. That hash then gets passed on to the next block, and so on, and so on. That continues on for all blocks in that blockchain. If for some reason, we had a nefarious individual, a bad actor, who goes and tries to manipulate or change the data on one of those blocks, it's then going to change the hash. That hash would then not match with the block on the subsequent block, and so on, and so on. Those things immediately appear, and it would get rejected from the blockchain. The other thing to consider is the fact that blockchain is a distributed ledger, and so we have many, many people that make up this blockchain community. There's lots of people that have copies of the blockchain, and They would need more than 50% consensus, in other words, the hacker would have to go in and manipulate all of those block chains on all of those different people's computers, and actually alter the hash and alter the hash of all the subsequent blocks across all the copies, or at least, more than 50% of those copies for that alteration to actually accepted; otherwise, it would be rejected from the blockchain, That makes it a very, very secure and virtually tamper resistant method of recording digital transactions and making everything very, very transparent. Some fundamental differences of encryption methods. Block versus stream. Now, what you'll need to understand here, is that both are actually symmetric. So don't get confused and think, well, block is symmetric and stream is asymmetric. No, they're both symmetric encryption methods. I'll block cipher, encrypts in chunks or blocks of data at a time, It's not doing it bit by bit. It does it in blocks at a time, whereas a stream cipher encrypts one bit at a time. It's doing it as the name implies, streaming, in that type of fashion. With the block cipher, let's say, for instance, here we have Bob and Alice again. They keep popping up here. Well, with a block cipher, it's a fixed length group, and so a fixed length group of bits or blocks. Each block of plain text has an equivalent size block of ciphertext. If I have a 64K block of plain text, I will have a 64K block of ciphertext. So here we see Bob and Alice communicating. In a stream cipher, we have encryption taking place bit by bit, using a pseudorandom cipher digit stream, otherwise known as a key stream. In that cipher stream, each plain text digit is encrypted, one at a time, bit by bit, with a corresponding digit of the key stream, and that gives us bit by bit digit of ciphertext. It's coming through as a stream. We take the message, and if I bring up our message here, we have our original plain text message. We have our own encryption method, in this case, a 128-bit secret key, and then our resultant, encrypted ciphertext message, so as that streams through, bit by bit, we'll take the very first bit of the message, encrypt it with the first bit of our key, and go to the next bit of the message with the next bit of the key, and that will go through, until the message is complete, and that gives us the resultant encrypted message on the opposite side. The recipient will then reverse that process and then decrypt that encrypted ciphertext back into plain text. Next, we have session keys. A session key is a single-use symmetric key. If you recall, symmetric keys are what? They're very fast, that's used for encrypting all the communication in one communication session. A symmetric key, as it mentioned, is faster than asymmetric, but it can also be used with asymmetric keys. We can have the best of both worlds. We can use an asymmetric key, a public/private key platform, to encrypt the session keys. If I want to communicate a large amount of data, and I don't want to have to use the overhead and the CPU cycles and all that stuff to generate all of that public key/private key cryptography for my entire communication session, what I can do is just encrypt the session key itself using that public key/private key. Then, on the recipient's side, they'll decrypt, get the session key, and then we can communicate using those session keys from that point forward.

Chapter 21 Asymmetric/Lightweight Encryption & Steganography

Next, let's talk about the differences between symmetric and asymmetric encryption. Symmetric encryption uses the same key, the symmetric on both sides, it's going to use that same key to both encrypt and decrypt a piece of data. Symmetric keys, as you might guess, are very fast. If, we have a secret key that's used on both the encryption and the decryption side of the equation here, so same key used for both. If I have my plain text, it goes through my encryption algorithm, secret key is applied, generates some cipher text, that cipher text is sent to the recipient, they use that same key, the same secret key to decrypt and revert that encrypted, or that cipher text, back into plain text. The same key is used for both encryption and decryption, often referred to as a shared key or a secret key encryption. Is far as concerns go, key management is really the biggest concern because both parties must know the secret key. It's also very difficult to prove identity. Because if you think about it, multiple people could know that secret key. If I need to communicate with multiple parties using this encryption platform, or this encryption algorithm, and I'm using the same key, well, if I have that shared among five different people, then I don't necessarily know which one of the five sent that message because any one of those could have used that key. But conversely, if I want to communicate in an encrypted fashion with more than one person and I don't want to use the same key for each communication session, then I'd have to manage multiple keys. That becomes unmanageable, especially at scale. Symmetric is faster than asymmetric because it's a single key for both encryption and decryption. Strength is also affected by the length of the key and the number of iterations you have to go through in the algorithm. In other words, how hard is that algorithm have to work in order to process and encrypt that data? The shorter is obviously faster, but it's less secure. Asymmetric encryption, on the other hand, uses a two-key system a public key and a private key. In that instance, I have two sides of the equation here, a sender and a recipient. The sender is going to encrypt that plain text with the recipient's public key. The sender has to have that recipient's public key ahead of time, so you'll share public keys amongst people that want to communicate. That public key is then used to encrypt that piece of data that result in cipher text. The recipient then uses their private key to decrypt what was encrypted with the public key. It's a two-key system here that are mathematically linked. The public key can encrypt something. The only thing that can decrypt that is the private key. That's where we get the two-key system from. Two keys, one public, one private. In that same situation, key pair, one for encryption, the other for decryption, a public key, as the name implies, is made publicly available, so you give that to anyone. They can then use that to encrypt data back to you. A private key, on the other hand, that must be kept secret. That must be guarded at all costs. Then either key can encrypt, or either key can decrypt, depending upon what we're doing. We can encrypt with the public key, and then decrypt with the private key. We can also encrypt with the private key and decrypt with the public key if we're doing digital signatures. Messages encrypted cannot be decrypted with the same key. That's why that we have this two-key-pair system. Public cannot do public just as private cannot do private. If you encrypt with the public, you have to decrypt with the private, and vice versa. Just understand that basic concept. Next, let's talk about lightweight cryptography. This is an encryption method that utilizes low computational power or energy consumption. NIST sponsored the effort in early 2018, and it's a small footprint and designed for constrained devices, in other words, IoT devices. It has AEAD specification, which means authenticated encryption with associated data, and it means the recipient of a message can use authentication to verify the integrity of both encrypted and unencrypted information within the message. This ensures that messages are coming from where they say they are, and the content of the message has not been altered in transit. The take away being, this is a type of cryptography that's used for devices that are very small in footprint, things that are constrained, meaning they have low computational power, perhaps low battery, or perhaps places where resources are minimal. It allows for some level of security within these IoT devices. Next we have steganography. Steganography lends itself to the old Trojan horse, where you can embed something inside of something else. Hiding a document inside of another document, it's not new, it's been around for quite a while, but it can be used very, very effectively, and it's very hard to detect. Documents can be hidden inside of other documents, such as MP3 files, image files, and video files. If someone wanted to put a secret message inside of an image file, as an example, they could use a tool to embed that specific message inside of an image file, send that image file to someone else. It would use the same tool to pull that text back out of the image. Steganography is very difficult to detect, but depending upon what they're embedding, it can bloat the file size quite a bit, so checking for excessively large files can help. If you have like a 30 MG image file, as an example, well, that may be indicative that, hey, there's something inside of that image file, when pretty much every other file is a tenth of that size. Those types of things can help, but it's not foolproof. Some popular steganography tools, and again, not an exhaustive list, so we have Xiao Steganography, we have image steganography, Steghide, Crypture, and then OpenStego. And there are many other ones out there, these are just a few that I happened to mentioned and want to call your attention to. As an example, here is a screenshot of OpenStego, and you can see we can either hide data or extract data. We can also digitally watermark stuff as well, but in this example we're going to hide data and then extract it. That's what I want to actually hide inside of a ping, or png. You can see I'm going to hide a text file inside of a graphic, a nature.png. That's the "cover" file. So once I do that, I'll put in the encryption algorithm, a password, and then I will hit the button to hide data. On the other side, the person I'm sending it to, they need to have that same tool. They also need to have OpenStego running on their machine on their side. From there, they will hit Extract Data. They will then open the graphic file that I sent them, the message.png, and from there, tell me where I'm going to output the message to and what's the password. Obviously, they're going to need to know what that password is. Once they do, it pulls that text file out of the image file and extracts it to whatever directory they choose. Next, we have the concept of homomorphic encryption. With this, there are three main concepts. We have partially homomorphic encryption, and this allows a select mathematical function, or set of functions, to be performed on encrypted values. One operation, either addition or multiplication, can be performed an unlimited number of times on the ciphertext, and I'll explain more of this in just a moment. Next, we have a somewhat homomorphic encryption. This is select mathematical functions to be performed, again, either addition or multiplication, but the operations can only be performed a set number of times. Then we have fully homomorphic encryption. This is developed from this SHE scheme, or the somewhat homomorphic encryption scheme, and is capable of both addition and multiplication, any number of times, and can make secure multiparty computation more secure. What do I mean by that? Where this starts to come into play is when we're talking about cloud security. Let's say, for instance, we have a cloud provider and we have a person who wants to put some type of an encrypted data into that cloud, but they want to be able to have other parties, whether it's programs, applications or people, work with that data or do something against that data, but not actually have access to the data. What it does, is allow people to perform computations against encrypted data without actually having access to the underlying data itself. In other words, without having to unencrypt the data first. Think of it as, you're putting data into a lockbox and you're locking it. It's a public key algorithm. You can give that public key to others. They can then actually do something with that data. They can work with it. It's almost like they're sticking their hand inside of a box and manipulating the data inside the box, but they're not allowed to take the data outside of the box. You're not allowed to actually see the end result. They can do some things to it, but they can't take it out. The person who put that data in is the only one who can actually retrieve it, so they can unlock the box and extract that data. It allows for someone to put data into the cloud securely, allow other things to work against or work on that data, I should say, securely, without actually having access to the underlying data. Encryption is never unencrypted. It doesn't leave that data vulnerable at any point in time. Let's look at some use cases for common types of encryption that we've talked about previously. We have a few things. We have low power devices, low latency, high resiliency, supporting confidentiality, supporting integrity, supporting obfuscation, supporting authentication, non-repudiation, and also resource versus security constraints. When we're talking about low power devices, ECC or Elliptical Curve Cryptography is a good example. It has low power consumption, which makes it well suited for providing security for mobile devices. For low latency, an example might be symmetric key cryptography. It provides quick or low latency, uses the same key as we talked about for both encryption and decryption, previously, it's also referred to as a secret key or a secret algorithm. Next for high resiliency, crypto systems that are made public. In other words, we're putting them out to the community and letting the community vet that actual algorithm and discover vulnerabilities. there's something referred to as Kerckhoffs'

Principle, and Auguste Kerckhoffs, who was a 19th century Dutch cryptographer, he stated or his principle states that a cryptosystem should be secure even if everything about the system, except the key, is public knowledge. Assuming that any system you develop will be immediately known to the adversary or to the person who's intercepting them, but it should still remain secure, even if they know everything about it, based upon the strength of the key. So getting back to our use cases, supporting confidentiality, well encryption in and of itself, that supports the confidentiality, because if we encrypt something, we're keeping it out of prying eyes, we're keeping it from being intercepted and then read. As far as integrity goes, supporting integrity, hashes is an example that supports or ensures integrity, especially with weaker algorithms like symmetric key cryptography. As we know, symmetric keys, they're fast, but they're also weaker. Then we have the same key using for both encryption and decryption. Hybrid cryptography uses symmetric, asymmetric and hashing to provide speed, confidentiality and also integrity. We can use asymmetric keys or the public key/private key to encrypt to the initial communication. Once that is decrypted, then we can include session keys or symmetric keys, which is then used to actually encrypt the data, . That gives us a speed, and then we can hash that information to make sure it hasn't been tampered with, which supports the integrity. As far as supporting obfuscation, obfuscation or hiding how something works is really the basis of cryptography. Creating a ciphertext that is extremely hard to reverse engineer or crack is the main thing through obfuscation. We're going to hide how that thing works. When it comes to supporting authentication, caching is used to authenticate a piece of data, ensuring nothing has changed during that transmission. We can compare two hashes to make sure that data has not been tampered with or manipulated in any way. If we take a hash of something before it's transmitted, and then take another hash once it's received, if those hashes match, then we can be sure that data has not been tampered with. As far as non-repudiation is concerned, Public Key Infrastructure, PKI, provides for non-repudiation through the use of public keys and private keys. Assuming the user keeps his private key secure, data encrypted via that private key could only originate from that user. It goes without saying that that's only really as secure as keeping the private key secure. If someone were to steal someone else's private key, they could encrypt data with that private key and make it appear as though that person sent it, and then, lastly, resource versus security constraints, right. This is an age old battle between making something very secure and the cost of speed, speed to market. Application developers are challenged with balancing security and the available resources - time, money, talent to ensure that applications are as secure as possible without undue burden to the actual application, to the deployment. It is a bit of a balancing act; however, it needs to be considered from the very beginning. Security should be not an afterthought, something that's tacked onto the very end; applications should be designed with security in mind from the very beginning.

Chapter 22 Cipher Suites, Random & Quantum Random Number Generators

We have strong versus weak ciphers. This is a point in time, a line in the sand type of thing because what was strong 5 years ago, 10 years ago, or considered strong, may be completely breakable today. It's really a matter of perspective and what tools are being used against that specific cipher. Computational resources and capabilities, as we know, they continue to increase. Every day we get more power, more capabilities. In fact, Moore's law states that every 18 months computing power doubles. Strong ciphers can become weak, or weaker at least, as computing power increases. A current example of strong ciphers would be AES, or the Advanced Encryption Standard, we have 3DES, and then Twofish. Actually, Blowfish should be incorporated in there as well, there hasn't been an effective cryptanalysis against the Blowfish as of yet. Those encryption algorithms are very strong. That's not to say, however, 5 years, 10 years down the road, as we really start to increase our computational power, whether it be quantum computing, whether it be big data, some type of distributed computing system, or perhaps a technology that hasn't even been invented yet, that computing power made just skyrocket, and then these encryption algorithms may be able to be broken in an instant. But as of today, these are considered strong ciphers. A weak cipher, by comparison, would be something like WEP, or the Wired Equivalency Protocol. When it first came out, it was considered a strong cipher; however, not too long thereafter it was broken, partly because of the RC4 initialization vector, and some other factors tied into that, but again, it went from being used everywhere to, uh-oh, we'd better not use that, let's replace it with something else. And as you recall, that went from WPA to WPA2, and then, WPA2-Enterprise if we're using it in an enterprise scenario and we want to use RADIUS or some other type of centralized authentication mechanism. Some things to be considering when you're looking at your own security infrastructure, the IoT devices in your network, the encryption algorithms. Some limitations that come to mind are things like speed. How fast can we encrypt, or how fast can something be decrypted? If we have very small or minimal resources, like certain IoT devices, we need a lightweight encryption to handle that. Things like size, the size of the keys could also, in turn, be weak keys. If we're using a weak encryption algorithm or the size of the key is too small, that could pose a security risk. Also, resource versus security constraints. We talked about IoT devices and how they have minimal resources, perhaps battery power or very small computational resources, small computational overhead, well, that can work against us, so lightweight encryption or a lightweight encryption algorithm should be chosen for those instances. If someone is able to take our data offline and then launch brute force attacks against that, they really have all the time in the world to try and crack that encryption algorithm. Conversely, if we're resource or overhead constrained, we may not have the time to actually create very strong keys as it would degrade or diminish the actual ability to stream data. And also, things like longevity, predictability. How predictable is their encryption algorithm? We talked a bit about random and pseudo-random number generators and also quantum key distribution. We'll talk more about that in just a moment. Things like computational overhead. We talked about IoT devices and how the minimal amount of computational overhead available to those devices creates a potential for security risk just because we don't have the ability to really create super strong keys, hence the lightweight cryptography that's being called for currently. Also, reuse, which comes into play in a number of different ways. Is an attacker able to reuse keys or replay information on the network? Are they able to discover or pick patterns in the encryption and perhaps gain insight into the data? And then also entropy, how random is that data? If we start off with pseudo random, as something that's very predictable, or using a weak key, then it's easier to crack. Because if it's built on, air quotes here, "a house of cards", it may look like it's secure, but in reality, it's not. If it's something that's not random enough, and we have enough time, computational power, resources to sit there and bang against that algorithm or actually launch computational attacks against that algorithm, given enough time, and if there is some predictability in that, we're able to discern how the encryption algorithm is started to begin with. And then from there, everything else falls apart. That's where things like random number generators, PRNGs, which is physical hardware, which is a random number generator, or pseudorandom number generators, which is software based, those things have varying degrees of security. But again, no matter what it is, given enough time, there will become some predictability in that device. The level of entropy, or unpredictability, low entropy is faster, but it's also weaker. Again, we're getting back to some of these limitations where speed might be a factor. Well, if we have to go very fast, we may not be able to get very, very random, so low entropy is faster, but it is weaker. High entropy, on the other hand, is slower, but it's more secure, so it's a trade-off. We have to decide what's most important when selecting an encryption algorithm. Possible attacks could be analysis of the PRNG output, the random number generator output. Or we could also have knowledge of the inputs. If we have knowledge of what's actually being inputted, or how things are started, it makes it much easier to understand the encryption that's coming out on the other side. Then lastly, if we're able to actually manipulate the inputs, well then, it makes it way easier to understand what's being encrypted and how that encryption algorithm works and makes it that much easier to break. That's where something like a quantum random number generator comes into play, which we currently have now, and will become more and more common as time goes on. We talked briefly about quantum key distribution, well, that's based around quantum random number generators. It uses the properties of quantum mechanics to create truly random numbers, because in quantum mechanics everything is completely random. There is no predictability, that output cannot be predicted, it would change every time. There is complete entropy, which means that the subsequent encryption is much more secure. In the coming years, expect a lot more from quantum computing, quantum random number generation, key distribution. In this chapter we talked about a lot of interesting topics. We talked about digital signatures, cipher suites, we talked about salting and hashing, also quantum communications and the various ways that takes place. We talked about Blockchain, how that works, the public ledgers. We talked about steganography, and how that can be used to hide things within other things, and then some common use cases and also limitations.

veryone that needs to be notified when that change begins and then notify when the changes end. And then if we have a maintenance call or a maintenance bridge setup, the teams that need to jump on and verify and then validate their applications and make sure that everything is back up and running before that maintenance window comes to a close.

Asset Management

It's very important from a compliance standpoint we understand how many of any one thing we have in the environment. As an example, if we have 5,000 servers, but we only bought 3,000 licenses or we have 500 instances of an application, but we only bought 2 copies, when it comes time to do a true up, that company comes in and asks to audit our environment. If we're not compliant, there could be a big, hefty fine associated with that or we have to quickly come up with the money to pay for the licenses and make things whole or remove those things out of the environment, which could create even more work and more effort. So it's important that asset management is properly maintained. Same thing when it comes to patching and updates. We need to have a clear understanding of how much of any one thing we have in the environment, whether it's Windows servers, Linux servers, IoT devices. All of these things need to be documented and understood in some type of asset management software so that we can quickly, at a glance, understand where we're deficient from a patching level of perspective, from an updates perspective. All of these things help to mitigate risk in the environment. It's hard to monitor what you don't know about. Asset management is a critical, critical component to a successful and secure system and an overall secure environment. In this chapter, we talked about personnel and the various things that we need to have in place to make sure our personnel is managed and administered properly. Also, we talked about the diversity of training techniques, third-party risk management, data classification, governance and retention, along with credential policies, and organizational policies, change management, asset management.

Conclusion

Congratulations on completing this book! I am sure you have plenty on your belt, but please don't forget to leave an honest review. Furthermore, if you think this information was helpful to you, please share anyone who you think would be interested of IT as well.

About Richie Miller

Richie Miller has always loved teaching people Technology. He graduated with a degree in radio production with a minor in theatre in order to be a better communicator. While teaching at the Miami Radio and Television Broadcasting Academy, Richie was able to do voiceover work at a technical training company specializing in live online classes in Microsoft, Cisco, and CompTia technologies. Over the years, he became one of the top virtual instructors at several training companies, while also speaking at many tech and training conferences. Richie specializes in Project Management and ITIL these days, while also doing his best to be a good husband and father.

www.ingramcontent.com/pod-product-compliance
Lightning Source LLC
Chambersburg PA
CBHW071243050326
40690CB00011B/2245